PLANE BASICS

Sam Allen

Sterling Publishing Co., Inc.   New York

Acknowledgments

My thanks go to the following individuals and companies for the help that they gave me in the preparation of this book:

Virginia Allen; Mark Johnson; Wayne Ruth; E.C.E. (Remscheid, Hasten, Germany); Record Tools Inc. (Pickering, Ontario, Canada); and Stanley Tools (New Britain, Connecticut).

METRIC EQUIVALENCY CHART

mm—millimetres   **cm—centimetres**

INCHES TO MILLIMETRES AND CENTIMETRES

inches	mm	cm	inches	cm	inches	cm
1/8	3	0.3	9	22.9	30	76.2
1/4	6	0.6	10	25.4	31	78.7
3/8	10	1.0	11	27.9	32	81.3
1/2	13	1.3	12	30.5	33	83.8
5/8	16	1.6	13	33.0	34	86.4
3/4	19	1.9	14	35.6	35	88.9
7/8	22	2.2	15	38.1	36	91.4
1	25	2.5	16	40.6	37	94.0
1 1/4	32	3.2	17	43.2	38	96.5
1 1/2	38	3.8	18	45.7	39	99.1
1 3/4	44	4.4	19	48.3	40	101.6
2	51	5.1	20	50.8	41	104.1
2 1/2	64	6.4	21	53.3	42	106.7
3	76	7.6	22	55.9	43	109.2
3 1/2	89	8.9	23	58.4	44	111.8
4	102	10.2	24	61.0	45	114.3
4 1/2	114	11.4	25	63.5	46	116.8
5	127	12.7	26	66.0	47	119.4
6	152	15.2	27	68.6	48	121.9
7	178	17.8	28	71.1	49	124.5
8	203	20.3	29	73.7	50	127.0

Library of Congress Cataloging-in-Publication Data

Allen, Sam.
    Plane basics / by Sam Allen.
        p.   cm.
    Includes index.
    ISBN 0-8069-8804-5
    1. Planes (Hand tools)   2. Woodwork.   I. Title.
TT186.A45 1993
684'.082—dc20
                                   93-24609
                                   CIP

10   9   8   7   6   5   4   3   2   1

Published by Sterling Publishing Company, Inc.
387 Park Avenue South, New York, N.Y. 10016
© 1993 by Sam Allen
Distributed in Canada by Sterling Publishing
% Canadian Manda Group, P.O. Box 920, Station U
Toronto, Ontario, Canada M8Z 5P9
Distributed in Great Britain and Europe by Cassell PLC
Villiers House, 41/47 Strand, London WC2N 5JE, England
Distributed in Australia by Capricorn Link Ltd.
P.O. Box 665, Lane Cove, NSW 2066
Manufactured in the United States of America

Contents

INTRODUCTION

The plane is one of the most basic of the woodworking tools. Planes can be used to transform the surface of a board from the initial rough-cut surface to a smooth, flat surface. They can also be used to joint the edge of a board, making it square and true. Specialized planes can be used to make grooves, dadoes, rabbets, and other joints. Planes can even be used to create intricate mouldings and decorative edges on a project. Because a plane removes a thin shaving of wood with each pass, it is unequalled when it comes to accurately trimming parts to fit. A plane that is properly maintained and sharpened is a joy to use, and the surface finish it produces can't be matched.

Modern power tools can perform many of the jobs previously done with planes, and yet the plane remains the tool of choice for many woodworkers. Practically every woodworker has at least one plane in his toolbox. The economic realities of the modern world dictate that most production work be done with power equipment, but for the amateur woodworker, enjoying the process of building a project is often as important as the finished product. For these woodworkers, using hand tools is one of the joys of woodworking. Even if you use power tools almost exclusively, there are times when only a hand plane will do the job. Even in a highly mechanized production shop, a plane is still used for the final trimming when doors are being fitted to a cabinet.

The woodworking plane has a long history. The name "plane" comes from the Latin word *planus*, which means level. Most ancient planes were made of wood, with the blade (called the iron) being the only metal part. There were exceptions, however. Iron-bodied planes were used in ancient Rome. Planes continued to evolve throughout the Middle Ages. At times, metal was used for the body of the plane; at other times, wood was used. By the 1700's, wooden planes were dominant and their design became somewhat standardized. These are the type of planes that I call *traditional* planes.

In this book, I classify planes into three groups (Illus. i-1). *Traditional* planes are planes with a wood body (called the stock) and a blade held in place with a wood wedge. *Transitional* planes have wood stocks, but have metal working parts that are used to secure and adjust the blade. *Metallic* planes are made almost entirely of metal, usually cast iron or brass.

Hazard Knowels is credited with the first patent for a plane with a cast-iron stock. The Knowels plane still used a wooden wedge to secure the blade. The Knowels patent was granted in 1827. In the years that followed, a number of inventors tried their hand at improving the method of adjusting the blade. Leonard Bailey eventually came up with the design that has become the standard used in most of today's planes. Bailey licensed many of his patents to the Stanley Rule and Level Company. Many of the classic Stanley planes are based on Bailey's designs.

Plane-making reached its zenith in the late 1800's–early 1900's. During this period, hundreds of different types of planes were available to perform practically any specialized task imaginable. Most of these planes remained in production until after World War II. The Stanley Company maintained one of the largest selections of specialized planes. The mass introduction of inexpensive power tools quickly eroded the market for these

Illus. i-1. In this book, I classify planes into three categories. As shown in this photograph, they are, from left to right: traditional planes, which have a wooden stock and an iron secured with a wooden wedge; transitional planes, which have a wooden stock, but an iron secured and adjusted with metal mechanical parts; and metallic planes, which are constructed almost entirely from metal (their handles are usually the only parts made from wood).

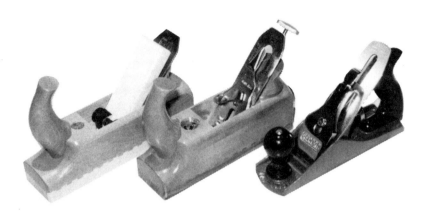

specialized planes. When Stanley discontinued its famous #55 plane in 1962, it marked the end of an era.

Today traditional wood planes, transitional planes, and metallic planes are all still available from several manufacturers, but not in the vast variety previously available. Since it is my intention that this book should be of benefit to the active woodworker who will actually put the planes to use, I have limited the scope of the book to planes that are currently being manufactured or, in a few cases, to planes that have been discontinued but were sold in large enough quantities that there are still many available on the used tool market. Recently, several small companies have started making reproductions of some of the discontinued planes.

Hand planes are generally safer to use than the corresponding power tools, but you still need to exercise caution and good sense when you use any tool. The cutting edge is very sharp. Handle the blade with care as you sharpen, install, or use it. When using any tool, you should be alert. Don't work if you are tired, upset, distracted or under the influence of drugs or alcohol.

One final note: As you read the information presented in the following pages, you will come across many general woodworking terms and some terms that pertain more specifically to using planes. If these terms are not defined in the text itself, turn to the glossary on pages 126–127. This glossary will help clarify some of the more confusing aspects of woodworking.

Sam Allen

Chapter I
USING BENCH PLANES

Bench planes are the most common type of plane. They are the planes used to smooth the face and edges of a board. Although the block plane is technically not classified as a bench plane, I have also included it in this chapter, because in practical use it performs many of the same jobs as the bench plane.

Before the mid-1800's, virtually all planes were made of wood. The plane iron was held in place with a wooden wedge. Depth-of-cut adjustments were made with a mallet. When metallic planes were introduced, wooden planes became less popular. Though this was partly to do with the "new is better" mentality, the ease of adjustment and the durability of the new metallic planes were a big advantage to a woodworker who used planes constantly. The advantage of a wooden plane is that the wooden sole glides more smoothly over the work. The transitional type of plane was made for the woodworker who didn't want to give up the appeal of a wooden stock, but who also wanted the ease of adjustment afforded by the new types of plane. In a transitional plane, a metal insert containing all of the blade adjustment parts is fit into a wooden stock.

Recently, there has been a resurgence of interest in wooden planes. A new generation of woodworkers has discovered the appealing feel of a wooden sole gliding over a board. Both traditional and transitional planes are available new. These new planes usually incorporate a sole made from one of the very hard woods like hornbeam or lignum vitae. This feature has reduced one of the drawbacks associated with the older planes. The soles of planes made from softer woods will eventually wear, widening the mouth and making the sole uneven.

The traditional plane with a wooden wedge seems at first to be harder to adjust than the newer types, but with a little practice you can learn to adjust it just as accurately.

By the late 1800's, metallic planes were becoming dominant. A metallic plane is usually made of cast iron, but brass is also used. The parts of metallic and wooden planes are discussed below.

Metallic Planes

Most modern metallic planes follow the design shown in Illus. 1-1. The stock (the body of the plane) is made from cast metal. The sides of the stock are called *cheeks*, and the bottom of the stock is called the *sole*. The front of the sole is called the *toe*, and the back is called the *heel*. The opening that the plane iron goes through is called the *throat*. The part of the throat that is visible on the sole of the plane is the *mouth*. The *handles* are usually made of wood. The rear handle is called the *tote*, and the front handle is called the *knob*.

The blade is called a *plane iron*. The term "plane iron" originated when the blade was the only iron part of the wooden plane. It can also be called the *blade* or *cutter*. The *cap iron* is attached to the top of the blade. It is often called the *chip breaker* or *plane iron cap*. It serves two functions. Its first job is to reinforce the blade, so as to

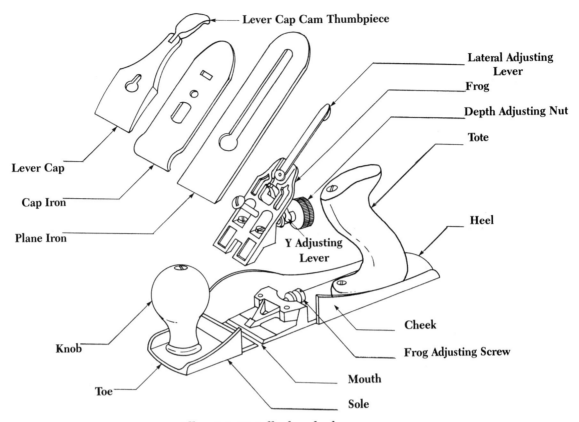

Illus. 1-1. Metallic bench plane.

prevent chatter. Chatter is an undesirable characteristic caused by flexing of the blade. When a blade chatters, it moves up and down repeatedly, causing a series of parallel ridges on the wood. The cap iron's other function is that of chip breaker. As the shaving climbs up from the cutting edge, it hits the cap iron. The curved end of the cap iron forces the shaving into a tight bend. This lessens the chance of tear-out. Tear-out occurs when the blade rips or tears out the grain of a workpiece.

The plane iron sits on the *frog*. The frog holds the blade at the proper angle and serves as the attachment point for the various parts used to adjust the blade. The frog position is adjustable. Moving the frog has the effect of changing the size of the throat. A small throat opening is desirable for taking fine cuts, while a wide throat permits deep roughing cuts.

The origin of the term "frog" is interesting. It is believed that it started as an inside joke at the Stanley Company. The original name for this part

was "bed piece." One of the workmen noted that the bed piece was inside the throat of the plane and remembered the old expression, "I have a frog in my throat." The name stuck, and was used unofficially for years. In 1898, Stanley used the term in its catalogue, and the name became official.

The *lever cap* holds the plane iron and plane iron cap assembly firmly against the frog. Lifting the *thumb piece* rotates the cam and releases the blade. The lever cap screw must be adjusted so that the blade is held firmly when the thumb piece snaps down.

The *lateral adjusting lever* is used to tilt the blade slightly from side to side. This adjustment is used to line up the cutting edge of the blade so that it projects uniformly from the mouth. Turn the plane upside down and sight across the cutting edge as you make this adjustment. Move the lever back and forth until the blade projects equally on both sides of the mouth. This will help prevent gouges made by the corners of the plane iron, and

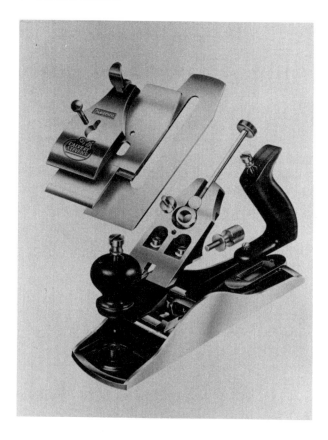

Illus. 1-2. The lead screw adjustment mechanism used in this plane eliminates most of the slack found in the Bailey adjustment mechanism. Also note the two-piece cap iron. This feature allows you to remove the lower section of the cap iron when sharpening the iron without disturbing the adjustment of the cap iron. When the plane is reassembled after sharpening, it will be adjusted exactly the same as it was before it was disassembled. This is convenient when it is necessary to sharpen the iron in the middle of a job. (Photo courtesy of Record Tools.)

the cut will be uniform in depth across the width of the plane.

The *depth adjusting nut* controls the depth of cut. Turning the nut moves the *Y adjusting lever*. The end of the adjusting lever fits into a slot in the plane iron cap. Turning the nut in pulls up the plane iron for a shallow cut. Turning it out pushes the plane iron down for a heavier cut. There is usually some slack in the mechanism. After adjusting the plane iron to the desired position, turn the nut out to take up any slack. This will prevent forward pressure on the plane iron from changing

Illus. 1-3. The parts of a traditional wooden bench plane.

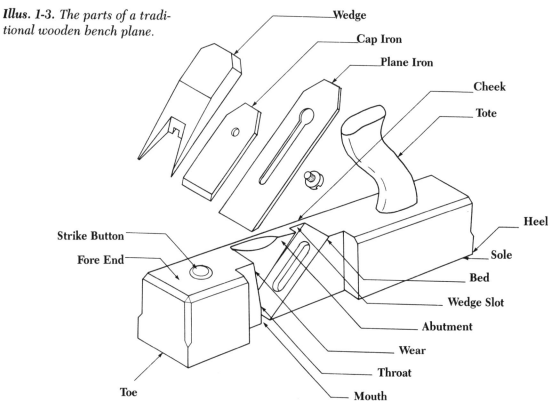

the adjustment. In Chapter 2, I will show you how to modify your plane to remove most of the slack.

Some bench planes use a different adjustment mechanism (Illus. 1-2). These planes have a lead screw adjustment that eliminates most of the slack found in the Bailey adjustment mechanism.

Wooden Planes

The parts of a traditional wooden plane are shown in Illus. 1-3. The wooden body of the plane is called the *stock*. The bottom of the stock is called the *sole*. A variety of woods can be used for the stock. Yellow birch, beech, and hornbeam are the most popular. The front of the stock is called the *fore end*. The opening in the stock where the plane iron is bedded and the shavings emerge is called the *throat*.

The sole can be an integral part of the stock, or it can be made of a harder wood. Lignum vitae is a very hard, durable wood that is used for the soles of expensive planes. It contains natural oils that give the sole a slick, waxy surface. Modern wooden planes often use intricate joints to attach the sole to the stock. The front of the sole is the *toe*, and the rear of the sole is the *heel*. The blade opening in the sole is the *mouth*. Some modern wooden planes have an adjustable mouth opening.

Planes that follow the German design have a long handle on the fore end called the *horn*. Planes that follow the English pattern usually have a handle at the rear called the *tote*, and no handle at the fore end. Most English-pattern planes have an open tote; large planes may have a closed tote, for added strength. Traditional planes come in many styles. Illus. 1-4 shows a few of the common types.

The blade is called a *plane iron*. The *wedge* holds the plane iron in place. The plane iron may have a slight taper. The taper causes the blade to wedge tighter as you make the cut. Some traditional planes don't have a cap iron. They use thicker blades that are less likely to flex and cause chatter. These planes are called *single-iron planes*. Many of the traditional planes that are made today do have a cap iron. They are called *double-iron planes*. The addition of the cap iron makes the plane less likely to produce tear-out, because the cap iron functions as a chip breaker.

The traditional way to secure the wedge is with two ledges on the cheeks of the throat opening. These ledges are called *abutments*. The end of the wedge is shaped to help the shavings clear the abutments, so that the plane won't become

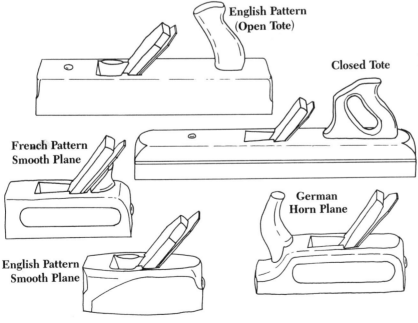

English Pattern
(Open Tote)

Closed Tote

French Pattern
Smooth Plane

English Pattern
Smooth Plane

German
Horn Plane

Illus. 1-4. There are many different types of traditional planes. This drawing shows a few of the more common ones.

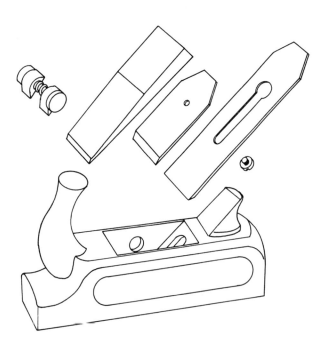

Illus. 1-5. This German horn plane uses an improved wedge-holding system that helps to clear the shavings from the throat more efficiently.

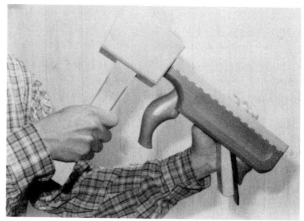

Illus. 1-6. The end of the plane iron can take on a mushroom shape from repeated blows. You can use another method of adjusting the depth, to avoid this. Lower the plane iron by tapping the toe end of the stock with a mallet.

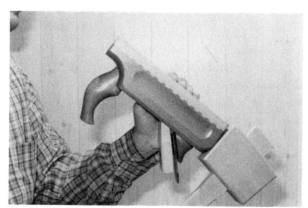

Illus. 1-7. To raise the blade for a fine cut, tap the heel end of the plane.

Illus. 1-8. After raising the plane iron, tap the wedge down to make sure that it is secure.

clogged with shavings. The E.C.E. company now offers an improved type of wedged plane. Instead of abutments, this type of plane uses a steel rod held in place with spring-loaded retainers. The shape of the wedge is very simple, and there is less chance that the plane will become clogged with shavings (Illus. 1-5).

Adjusting a traditional plane can seem mysterious at first, but it is really quite simple. Using traditional terminology, a plane iron that is set to take a heavy cut is set "rank"; when it is set to take a shallow cut, it is set "fine." To lower the plane iron for a rank cut, tap the back of the plane iron with a mallet or a hammer. If you hold the plane with its sole up and sight down the sole as you tap on the blade, you can see how much of the blade is exposed. If you look at an old plane, the end of the plane iron usually has a mushroom shape that is caused from repeated blows. You can use another method of adjusting the depth, to avoid this. Lower the plane iron by tapping the toe end of the stock with a mallet (Illus. 1-6). This is a method preferred by many, because it means that you don't have to hit the plane iron at all. Lateral adjustments can be made by tapping the sides of the plane iron.

To raise the blade for a fine cut, tap the heel end of the plane (Illus. 1-7). Most modern wood planes have a metal strike button in the heel so you won't damage the stock. Older planes may have a hardwood strike button or no strike button at all. Long planes may have the strike button located on the top of the fore end. Hitting the top of the fore end of a plane has the same effect of raising the iron.

After raising the plane iron, tap the wedge down to make sure that it is secure (Illus. 1-8). A light tap is all that is necessary. Overtightening the wedge can damage the plane or make it difficult to adjust. Tightening the wedge will lower the blade slightly, so you have to raise the blade a little more than necessary to compensate for this. Adjusting a traditional plane takes practice, because you have to learn just how much movement to allow for and how hard to tap. But once you get the feel of tapping the plane, it is not difficult.

Transitional planes use metal adjustment mechanisms to make them as easy to adjust as metallic planes (Illus. 1-9). Older transitional planes frequently have an iron insert that contains all of the adjustment mechanism.

Modern transitional planes may use a different type of adjustment mechanism, as shown in Illus. 1-10. This type of adjusting mechanism is spring-loaded to eliminate any slack in the adjustment. This is called zero backlash. It means that when you make an adjustment there is no slack to take up before the plane iron begins to move.

Illus. 1-9. Transitional planes use metal adjustment mechanisms to make them as easy to adjust as metallic planes. Older transitional planes frequently have an iron insert that contains all of the adjustment mechanism, as can be seen on the plane at the rear of this photograph. The plane in front is a modern transitional plane.

Illus. 1-10. This cross section shows the adjustment mechanism of a modern transitional plane made by the E.C.E. company. This type of adjusting mechanism is spring-loaded, to eliminate any slack in the adjustment. This is called zero backlash.

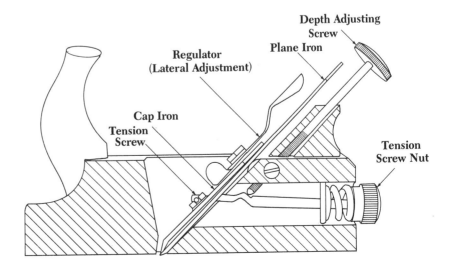

Types of Plane

There are many different types of plane. In this chapter, I will discuss the most common types. These are general-purpose planes that are used for preparing and finishing lumber and trimming parts for assembly. Other types of specialty planes are covered in Chapters 5 and 6. While the sizes of wooden planes can vary greatly, the size of metallic planes is fairly standardized (Table 1-1).

TABLE 1-1

Name	Width of Plane Iron	Length of Sole
Smooth 03	1¾"	9"
Smooth 04	2"	9¾"
Smooth 04½	2⅜"	10¼"
Jack 05	2"	14"
Jack 05½	2⅜"	14¾"
Fore 06	2⅜"	18"
Jointer 07	2⅜"	22"
Jointer 08	2⅝"	24"

Most of the planes covered in this chapter are called bench planes. They are called bench planes because they are usually used at the workbench to surface and joint stock. The jack, fore, trying, jointer, and smoothing planes discussed below are all bench planes. Bench planes have the plane iron set at a high angle, and the bevel side of the plane iron faces downwards. The other type of plane discussed in this chapter is the block plane.

Block Plane

The block plane is a small plane that fits in the palm of your hand (Illus. 1-11). It is used primarily for trimming. Legend has it that the block plane is so named because it was originally used by butchers to dress the top of their chopping blocks.

The block plane's biggest advantage is its small size. It is ideal for trimming with one hand while you hold the work with the other hand. It is often used by carpenters because it is easy to carry around the job site. Carpenters typically use the block plane to trim joints on interior trim and to fit cabinets and wood panelling. The block plane is ideal for planing to a scribed line when fitting a

Illus. 1-11. The block plane is a small plane that fits in the palm of your hand. It is used primarily for trimming. The block plane's biggest advantage is its small size. It is ideal for trimming with one hand, while you hold the work with your other hand. This photograph shows, from left to right, a traditional wooden block plane, a transitional wooden block plane, and a metallic block plane.

panel or cabinet to an irregular wall. Cabinetmakers often use a block plane to trim joints and trim doors and drawers to fit the opening.

A block plane can be tuned so that it will make a good finishing cut. A finishing plane is used instead of sandpaper to give wood its final finished surface before a finish is applied. See Chapter 2 for information on tuning a plane.

The metallic block plane differs from bench planes in that the plane iron is bedded at a lower angle and the bevel on the blade faces up. Wooden block planes are designed more like other bench planes. The blade is positioned bevel-down. Some wooden block planes have the blade bedded at a high 50-degree angle. This is called "York pitch." It makes the plane cut smoother on hard woods with a highly figured grain.

For best results when using a block plane, adjust the blade so it barely projects out of the mouth. Use a series of light strokes to remove the wood. Although it is often said that a block plane is best for planing end grain, my experience has shown that a good smooth plane is really better for planing end grain. Most block planes tend to chatter when used on end grain, because the blade is not supported as well as it is in a bench plane. When trimming end grain, work in from both edges towards the middle to prevent splitting off a splinter as the plane crosses the edge. If it is impossible to plane from both edges, clamp a backup block of scrap wood to the far edge.

Jack Plane

The jack plane can range in length from 12 to 17 inches (Illus. 1-12). Usually, it is about 14 inches long. The jack plane evolved from a plane called the fore plane. The fore plane received its name because it was used before any other plane when rough lumber was being surfaced. Carpenters using the fore plane found that it was slightly too long to carry comfortably around the job site, so they frequently shortened the plane. "Jack" is a carpenter's term for shortened; just as a jack rafter is a shortened rafter at a hip or valley in a roof, a jack plane is a shortened fore plane.

The jack plane has superseded the fore plane as the first plane to be used on rough lumber. It is used to remove the saw marks and cut down high spots; then a longer plane is used to make the surface true and flat. Besides dressing rough lumber, the jack plane can be used for trimming to size and jointing the edges of short boards.

The jack plane can be used diagonally across the grain for rough cutting, and parallel to the grain for finer cuts. When used to make deep roughing cuts, the cutting edge of a jack plane should be ground slightly convex (shaped like the exterior of a circle); this is called a cambered edge. Today, the

Illus. 1-13. A cambered cutting edge allows the plane to take a deep cut for removing a lot of wood quickly, but the surface will have pronounced waves. Other planes with a straight cutting edge must be used to further smooth the surface.

jack plane is regarded by the manufacturers as a multi-purpose plane, so the cutting edge is usually ground straight at the factory. One exception is the scrub plane.

The scrub plane is a short jack plane. It is usually used as the first step when dressing the face of rough lumber. The plane iron is ground convex. This camber makes it easy to take deep roughing cuts.

The scrub plane is used to remove a lot of wood quickly. In most cases, the scrub plane is pushed diagonally across the grain at about a 45-degree angle. The surface left by the scrub plane has pronounced waves due to the cambered cutting edge (Illus. 1-13). Other planes must be used to further smooth the surface. The main purpose of the scrub plane is to rough-out the wood close to its final dimensions and to remove large bumps and warps in the board.

Only wooden scrub planes are presently available. If you want a metallic plane to do the same job, regrind the plane iron so that it has a cambered edge. Set the frog back to open the throat and set the cap iron 1/16 inch back from the cutting edge. See Chapter 2 for details on making these modifications.

Illus. 1-12. The jack plane ranges in length from 12 to 17 inches. Shown on the left is a traditional German jack plane; on the right is a metallic Bailey-type jack plane. The name "jack" is a carpenter's term for shortened; the jack plane evolved from a shortened fore plane.

Fore, Trying, and Jointer Planes

The fore plane, the trying plane, and jointer are long planes, ranging from 18 to 36 inches in length. These planes are used to make a surface perfectly flat. The long sole rides on top of the high spots and slices them off without dipping into the low spots. Long planes can be used to flatten and clean up the face of a board when rough lumber is being dressed. When making the first cuts, use the plane to cut diagonally across the grain; then cut parallel to the grain, to smooth the surface.

These planes are currently available in both metallic and wooden types. The metallic type is simply an elongated version of a standard Bailey design. The long sole of a metallic plane can produce a lot of friction, making it difficult to push. A corrugated sole offers less resistance and, when used on green wood or wood with a lot of sap, doesn't stick or gum up as often (Illus. 1-14). Many woodworkers prefer a long plane with a wooden sole, because it glides over the board more easily. Wooden planes are also lighter; this can be an advantage in a plane this large. The design of a long wooden plane differs slightly from the shorter planes. Note the closed tote shown in Illus. 1-15; it almost looks like the handle of a saw.

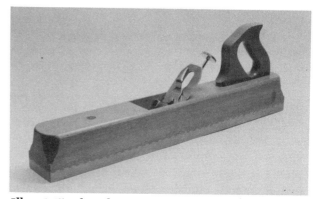

Illus. 1-15. The advantages of a wooden plane are most apparent when a long plane is used. Wooden planes are lighter and easier to push than their metallic counterparts. Long wooden planes like this transitional trying plane often have a closed tote.

The fore plane is about 18 inches long. As explained above, it was originally the first plane used when surfacing rough lumber. The fore plane is still ideally suited for this job. Because it is longer than the jack plane, it will flatten the surface better. When used to make roughing cuts, its cutting edge should be cambered, as explained in the section on jack planes.

A trying plane is 20 to 24 inches long. It is used to flatten the surface of a board and remove the wavy marks left by the jack or fore plane. The process of flattening the face of a board is called "trying." The cutting edge of a trying plane can be ground with a very slight camber to prevent the corners from digging into the face of the board.

The jointer is 22 to 36 inches long. For most uses, a 24-inch jointer is most practical. The jointer is designed for jointing an edge. Jointing is the process of making an edge straight and square with the face of the board. The cutting edge of a jointer plane should be ground straight across.

There is very little difference between fore planes, trying planes, and jointers. Today, most come from the factory with a straight cutting edge, so if you want a cambered cutting edge, you'll have to grind it yourself. I have found that the long plane I use most often is a 24-inch-long transitional wooden trying plane (Illus. 1-16). I grind the cutting edge straight, so it can do the work of a jointer, and I round off the corners of the cutting edge so it won't gouge the wood when

Illus. 1-14. Long metallic planes like the fore and jointer planes often have corrugated soles. Here the plane on top has a standard sole, and the one on the bottom has a corrugated sole. The corrugated sole helps to reduce friction, so the plane is easier to push.

Illus. 1-16. A 24-inch-long trying plane is the most versatile of the long planes. If you grind the cutting edge straight and round the corners, it can do the work of a fore plane and a jointer.

Illus. 1-17. The smooth plane is 9 to 10 inches long. It is used to give the wood a final smoothing after other planes have been used to flatten the surface. The plane on the left is a German transitional smooth plane. The plane on the right is a metallic smooth plane.

doing the work of a trying plane. If the board is fairly flat and not much wood has to be removed, you can use a trying plane set up this way to remove the rough saw marks from the board by making diagonal strokes across the grain. This prepares the board for the final flattening, at which time you can push the plane parallel to the grain.

Smooth Plane

The smooth plane is 9 to 10 inches long (Illus. 1-17). Its cutting edge is ground straight, not cambered. It is used primarily after the wood has been flattened by the other planes. It is often called a smoothing plane because it is used for smoothing the surface of a board.

The smooth plane is a finishing plane—it is used to give the wood a final smooth finish. A sharp smooth plane can give the wood a smooth shiny surface that cannot be equalled with sandpaper. When a board is properly planed with a smooth plane, there is no need for sanding. If there are small imperfections in the surface left from the planing operation, they can be removed with a cabinet scraper (see Chapter 7).

If you buy your lumber surfaced from the mill, you can get by without some of the other planes, but a smooth plane is still necessary to remove the mill marks left on the boards. Mill marks are the wavy patterns left by the rotating cutter of the thickness planer. They are difficult to remove by sanding, because the sandpaper follows the surface of the board too closely. A smooth plane rides on top of the crest of the waves and slices them off.

If you are trying to decide which plane to purchase first, I suggest a smooth plane. It is a good choice if you will only have one plane, because it is versatile and easy to use. It won't flatten an edge as accurately as a jointer would, but it produces a very smooth surface and is excellent for trimming. Even though many woodworkers regard a block plane as the best tool for trimming, the smooth plane is also effective. It will even trim end grain, if you are careful to work in from both ends, and is light enough to use with one hand.

My first plane was a smooth plane. I got it when I was 12 years old. I have used it continuously since, and it is still one of my favorite planes.

Planing Techniques

Securing the Work

To plane effectively, you must use two hands, so you should find a means for securing the work. A good workbench makes planing easier. The ideal bench height for planing is 30 inches, but since this is too low for other activities, most benches have a height of about 34 inches. I have fitted my bench with a number of useful stops and dogs to make it easy to secure a variety of boards (Illus. 1-18).

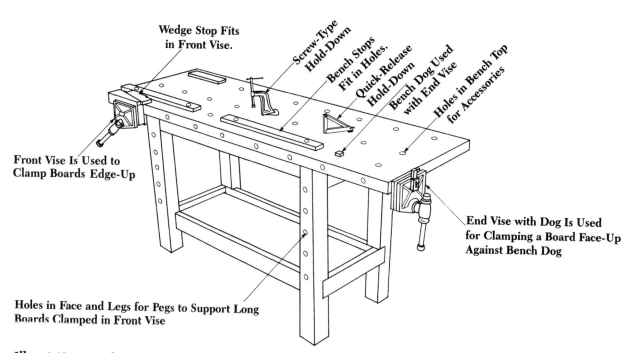

Wedge Stop Fits
in Front Vise.

Screw-Type
Hold-Down

Bench Stops
Fit in Holes.

Quick-Release
Hold-Down

Bench Dog Used
with End Vise

Holes in Bench Top
for Accessories

Front Vise Is Used to
Clamp Boards Edge-Up

End Vise with Dog Is Used
for Clamping a Board Face-Up
Against Bench Dog

Holes in Face and Legs for Pegs to Support Long
Boards Clamped in Front Vise

Illus. 1-18. A good workbench is necessary to plane effectively. This illustration shows several bench accessories that are useful for holding boards when planing.

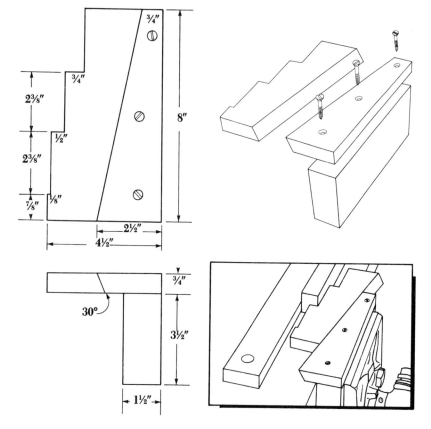

Illus. 1-19. This wedge stop holds the board securely because forward pressure from the plane wedges the board tighter. To release the board, tap the wedge with a mallet. You can make a wedge stop from these plans. Use a hardwood. The tail of the outside part of the stop fits into a bench vise. The board is wedged against a long bench stop that fits into holes in the bench top.

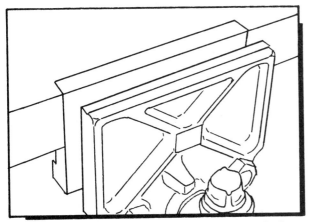

Cut vise into face of bench so that its inside jaw is flush with the bench face. Long boards will be supported better when they can rest flat against the bench.

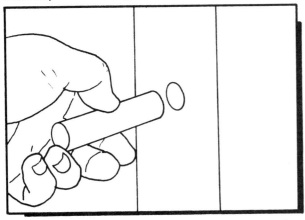

Pegs fit into holes in bench face and legs. They are used to support long boards clamped in the vise.

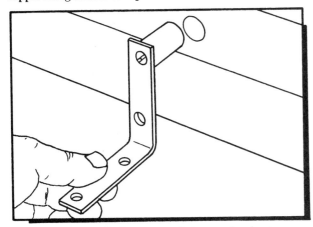

The bracket is made from an angle iron and a short dowel. It is sized so that when placed in the top row of holes, the bottom of the bracket is level with the bottom of the vise.

Illus. 1-20. Another type of support.

When planing the edge of a board, you can simply clamp it in the vise. I have cut the front of my bench to let in the vise, so that the inside face of the jaw is flush with the front edge of the bench. This helps to support the board. I also drilled a series of holes in the front edge of the bench and the front legs to accept a peg to hold up the end of a long board. I also use another type of support, made by attaching an angle iron to a piece of dowel (Illus. 1-20). (An angle iron is a piece of steel that is L-shaped.)

I have made a wedge stop that I like to use when planing several boards. A light tap with a mallet secures or releases the board (Illus. 1-19).

For planing the face of a board, I use a bench stop at the end of the bench and one along the side of the board, or I clamp the board between the end vise and a dog placed in one of the holes in the bench top.

Holding the Plane

Hold a metallic plane as shown in Illus. 1-2. If your hand is too large to fit around the tote comfortably, grip the tote and extend your index finger along the side of the blade. Illus. 1-22 shows the proper grip for a wooden horn plane, a plane with a horn instead of a knob. Many wooden planes don't have a horn or a knob. To hold this type of plane, grasp the fore end of the plane with your thumb on one side and your fingers on the other. Turn your hand so that your palm is facing towards the toe of the plane. This looks awkward, but it works much better than the other way because your wrist is free to pivot back and forth (Illus. 1-23). For edge-jointing, wrap your fingers around the toe of the plane as shown in Illus. 1-24. Your fingertips then become a fence that helps to guide the plane along the edge.

Planing Stance

The next step is to get into the proper stance for planing (Illus. 1-25). You will do a better job and it will be less tiring if you put your whole body to work, instead of just your arms. Stand close to the work, with your shoulders directly above the board. Place one foot forward below the board, with your leg slightly bent. Your other leg should

Illus. 1-21. This is the proper grip for a metallic plane. If your hand is too large to fit comfortably on the tote, as shown here, you can extend your index finger and rest it against the side of the blade.

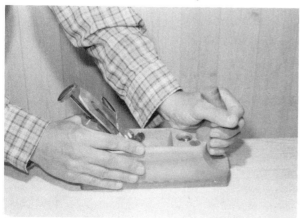

Illus. 1-22. This is the proper grip for a wooden horn plane.

Illus. 1-23. Wooden planes that don't have a horn or knob should be gripped this way. The hand on the fore end should be rotated palm forward. This gives your wrist more freedom of motion.

Illus. 1-24. When jointing an edge, wrap your fingers under the sole of the plane to help guide it. Let your fingertips rub lightly against the face of the board. This technique should only be used when the face of the board has been planed smooth. If the face is rough, keep your hand on top of the plane, to avoid getting a splinter in your fingers.

Illus. 1-25. The proper stance for planing. Stand close to the work, with your shoulders directly above the board. Place one foot forward below the board with your leg slightly bent. Your other leg should be straight, with your foot slightly behind your body.

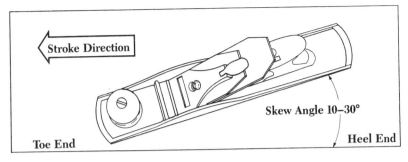

Illus. 1-26. *Skewing the plane gives its cutting edge more of a slicing action. For most work, a 10-degree skew works well. For boards with difficult grain, you can skew the plane up to 30 degrees.*

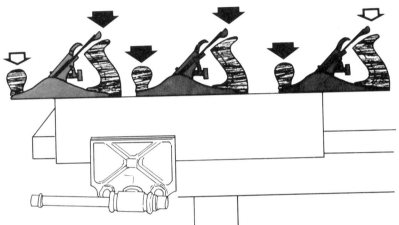

Illus. 1-27. *As you start the stroke, put most of the downward pressure on the knob. When the entire sole is on the board, maintain an even downward pressure on the plane as you push the plane along the board. As the plane nears the toe end of the board, release some of the pressure on the knob and maintain the downward pressure on the tote.*

be straight, with your foot slightly behind your body so that your two feet are separated by the distance they would normally be when you walk. In this position, you can rock your whole body back and forth as you make the cut.

Throughout this book, I will be using the terms *toe end* and *heel end* to designate the two ends of a board. The designations are to simplify the directions and are dependent on the direction that the plane is facing. When you place the plane on the board, the toe end of the board is the end in front of the toe of the plane. The heel end of the board is the end behind the heel of the plane.

Place the toe of the plane on the heel end of the board and slightly skew the plane. This means that you angle the plane slightly, but leave the entire length of its sole still on the board (Illus. 1-26). For most work, a 10-degree skew works well. For boards with difficult grain, you can skew the plane up to 30 degrees. As you start the stroke, put most of the downward pressure on the knob. When the entire sole is on the board, maintain an even downward pressure on the plane as you push the plane along the board. For long

boards, you will need to walk forward as you make the cut. As the plane nears the toe end of the board, release some of the pressure on the knob and maintain the downward pressure on the tote (Illus. 1-27). Lift the plane off the work after its mouth has passed the end of the board. Don't pull the plane rearwards with the iron in contact with the wood because it will dull the cutting edge.

When you are done with the plane, lay it down on its side on the bench. Woodworkers consider it poor technique to lay a plane down on its sole. Laying the plane down on its side keeps its cutting edge away from any grit on the bench top that could dull it. When you store a plane on a shelf, you can place it on its sole if you attach a narrow strip of wood to the shelf where the heel of the plane will rest. This will raise the sole enough to keep the cutting edge off the shelf.

Grain Direction

Grain direction is very important when you are planing. Small changes in grain direction will become apparent as you plane. Illus. 1-28 shows how the grain intersects the wood surface at an angle.

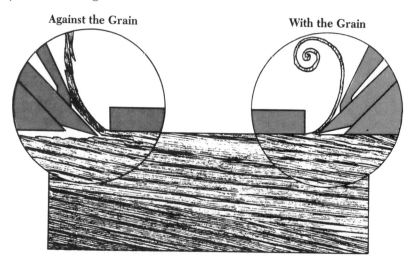

Illus. 1-28. Grain direction is very important when you are planing. Small changes in grain direction will become apparent as you plane. This illustration shows how the grain intersects the wood surface at an angle. The arrow shows the direction to move the plane with the grain.

The arrow shows the direction to move the plane with the grain. Illus. 1-29 shows how the plane slices off the wood fibres when cutting with the grain, and what can happen when you plane against the grain. The wood splits along the grain, leaving a chipped surface; this is called tear-out. If you experience this, turn the board around and plane from the other direction. Planing with the grain is sometimes called planing uphill. When viewed from the side, the grain looks like the slope of a hill. When you are planing in the proper direction, the plane is travelling in the uphill direction.

Stock that is straight-grained and free of knots is easy to plane. The shavings will come off in long

Illus. 1-29. The plane slices off the wood fibres when cutting with the grain (right enlarged view). When you plane against the grain (left enlarged view), the wood splits along the grain, leaving a chipped surface.

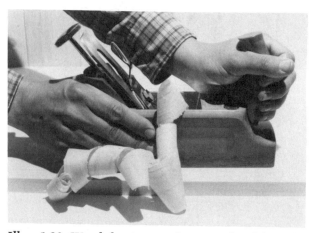

Illus. 1-30. Wood that is straight-grained and free of knots is easy to plane. The shavings will come off in long unbroken curls.

unbroken curls (Illus. 1-30). Problems occur when the grain direction changes in the board. This is particularly a problem around knots, but it can occur anywhere in the board. The plane will be cutting fine with the grain, when suddenly the grain direction changes and the wood starts to chip. This problem is called tear-out. Sometimes tear-out can be avoided by keeping the plane iron sharp and the mouth opening small. It may be necessary to stop and change directions if the tear-out is severe. The grain in highly figured woods changes direction frequently. In this case, use a well-tuned plane and take a very shallow cut. Holding the plane skewed can help when planing around knots. Skewing the plane helps the iron slice the wood fibres off.

Adjusting the Plane

The plane will have to be adjusted for the job at hand. (Adjusting the plane is fully discussed in Chapter 3.) For rough hogging cuts, the iron is set rank. For the final smoothing, set the iron fine. I like to start with the plane adjusted for a very fine cut, and then increase the cut as necessary until the desired depth of cut is reached. Make a pass over the wood and look at the surface. If the surface is smooth, adjust the plane for a deeper cut. If there are chatter marks, the cut is too rank. If chattering occurs even when the plane is set fine, then there is a problem with the way the iron is bedded. See Chapter 3 for details on bedding the iron.

If there is tear-out, then set the cap iron closer to the cutting edge. On planes that have an adjustable frog or mouth opening, making the mouth smaller will also help prevent tear-out.

If the plane chokes with shavings, the plane may be set too rank. The problem could also be caused by having the cap iron too close to the cutting edge. The chip breaker can cause the shavings to curl up too tight and get wedged in the throat.

When a plane "writes its name on the wood," it is leaving gouges or lines on the surface. If the lateral adjustment is not correct, one corner of the iron will gouge the wood. Turn the plane sole-up and sight across the cutting edge. Move the lateral adjustment lever until the cutting edge is parallel with the sole. A nicked cutting edge can also cause the plane to write its name. If you see a nick, it's time to resharpen the iron. Refer to Chapter 2 for sharpening instructions.

When the plane is adjusted for the job and cutting smoothly, you're ready to start working.

Dressing Rough Lumber

Today, most woodworkers either buy lumber that has been surfaced at the mill or use power equipment to surface rough lumber. A power jointer is used to achieve a flat face, and the thickness planer is used to plane the board to its correct thickness.

If you want to surface lumber in the traditional way, use hand planes. One big advantage of surfacing your own lumber is that you can vary the thickness to suit the project. Many antiques are made from lumber that is slightly thicker than the standard ¾-inch-thick lumber available today. The actual thickness varies from one project to another, but it is usually close to ⅞ inch. If you start with 1-inch-thick rough lumber, you can usually get a ⅞-inch-thick surfaced board unless there is a lot of warp to take out. (Warping is a bow, cup, or twist in a board.)

Some projects call for lumber that is thinner than ¾ inch; in this case, you can start with ¾-inch-thick lumber and plane it thinner. Although it is hard work, it is very satisfying to have worked a board from its rough state to a finished project entirely with hand tools.

Unless you will need the length in the finished project, cut the boards into shorter lengths to surface them. Their lengths will be dependent on the parts you plan on cutting from the boards, but boards four to six feet long will fit on the bench comfortably and work out well.

Now, decide which side of the board you will designate as the *face*, or good side of the board. All other measurements will be taken from the face. Place the board face-up on the bench with the end against a bench stop, or clamp it between the end vise and a bench dog.

Use a long straightedge to check for high spots in the length of the board (Illus. 1-31). (A straightedge is a piece of material with a straight edge for testing straight lines and surfaces or using straight lines.) A straightedge across the face will show any cupping (Illus. 1-32). Use winding sticks to check the board for twist (Illus. 1-33). Winding sticks are simply two boards that are the same size and have straight edges. They are longer than the width of the board, to exaggerate the twist in the board. Place one winding stick at each end of the board, and then sight across the two sticks. If the edges aren't parallel, then the board is twisted.

You now have a good idea of where the high spots are in the board, and you can begin planing.

Illus. 1-31. Use a long straightedge to check for high spots in the length of the board. Do this before beginning to plane, to get an idea of how much wood will have to be removed and, occasionally during the planing process, to check your progress.

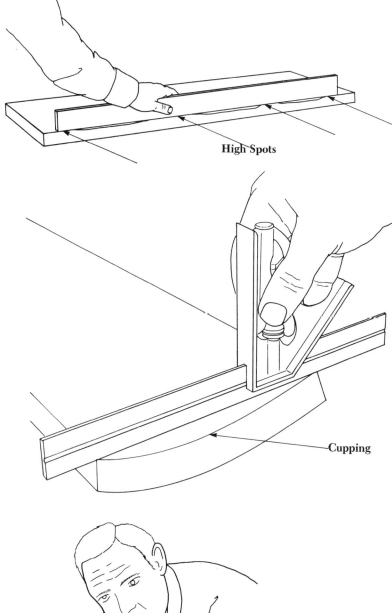

High Spots

Illus. 1-32. A straightedge across the face will show any cupping.

Cupping

Illus. 1-33. Use winding sticks to check the board for twist. Winding sticks are two boards that are the same size and have straight edges. They are longer than the width of the board, to exaggerate the twist in it. Place one winding stick at each end of the board and then sight across the two sticks. If the edges aren't parallel, then the board is twisted. Recheck the board after you have planed it, to make sure you removed all of the twist.

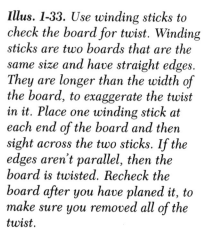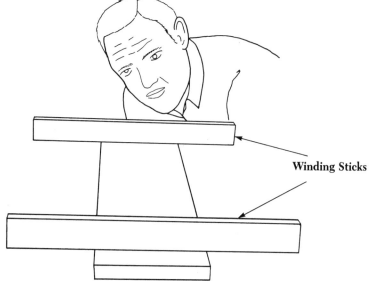

Winding Sticks

In many cases, you can do the entire job with a trying plane. But when the high spots will require a lot of stock removal to bring them down, start with a scrub plane. The scrub plane is designed to remove a lot of stock quickly. Its cambered cutting edge makes it efficient, and the wavy pattern it leaves will be planed out later. For this operation, I like to plane across the board at a 45-degree angle (Illus. 1-34). Cutting at an angle to the grain helps to prevent tear-out when you make heavy cuts. My bench has holes for a bench stop that the side of the board can rest against, to facilitate this operation.

Continue until most of the high spots have been worked down. A jack or a fore plane can also be used for the initial planing to work down high spots and remove the rough saw marks. If its cutting edge is ground with a camber and its blade is set rank, a jack or a fore plane will remove the high spots and saw marks just as quickly as a scrub plane. Also, the longer length of the sole on these planes flattens the surface better, so there is less work to do with the trying plane (Illus. 1-35).

If the board is fairly flat and not too rough, you can do the entire job with a trying plane. Begin by setting the plane rank and making the cuts across the grain at a 45-degree angle. Continue until the surface is flat and the saw marks have been removed.

The final flattening is done with a trying plane (Illus. 1-36). For this operation, make a lighter cut and move the plane in a straight line with the grain. As you start the cut, put more downward pressure on the toe of the plane; but once the plane is entirely on the board, apply more pressure to the heel. This will make the plane cut flat and avoid any tendency to taper off the ends. Plane along the entire face until you are cutting an even shaving all along the length of the board. The surface should now be flat and true. Make a mark on the face, to designate it for later reference. Illus. 1-37 shows the traditional mark used to designate the face; the tail of the mark points to the edge that will be used as a reference edge.

The final step in dressing the surface is to use a smooth plane to remove all planing marks and make the surface perfectly smooth (Illus. 1-38).

Illus. 1-34. When the high spots will require a lot of stock removal to bring them down, start with a scrub plane. The scrub plane is designed to remove a lot of stock in a hurry. Plane across the board at a 45-degree angle. Planing at an angle to the grain helps to prevent tear-out when you make heavy cuts.

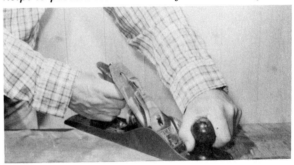

Illus. 1-35. A jack or a fore plane can also be used for the initial planing to work down high spots and remove the rough saw marks. If it has a cambered cutting edge, a jack or a fore plane will remove the high spots and saw marks just as quickly as a scrub plane. The longer length of the sole will flatten the surface better than the sole on a scrub plane.

Illus. 1-36. The final flattening is done with a trying plane. Make a light cut and move the plane in a straight line with the grain. Plane along the entire face until you are cutting an even shaving all along the length of the board. The surface should now be flat and true.

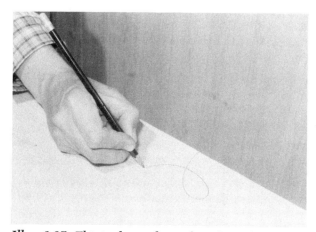

Illus. 1-37. This is the traditional mark used to designate the face; the tail of the mark points to the edge that will be used as a reference edge.

Illus. 1-38. The final step in dressing the surface is to use a smooth plane to remove all planing marks and make the surface perfectly smooth. You may want to wait to do this until later in the project-making process, so you don't mar the final surface during the initial stages of construction.

Illus. 1-39. Set a marking gauge for the desired thickness and gauge all around the board with the gauge's fence on the planed face.

You may want to wait to do this until later in the project-making process, so you don't mar the final surface during the initial stages of construction.

Set a marking gauge for the desired thickness and gauge all around the board with the gauge's fence on the planed face (Illus. 1-39). (A marking gauge is used to lay out lines parallel to the edges of a board.) Now, plane the surface down to the gauged lines. If much stock must be removed, use the scrub plane as described above. Do the final surfacing with the trying plane. Use this same technique when you want to thin down a board. For example, if you need ½-inch-thick boards for drawer sides, but you only have ¾-inch-thick lumber on hand, you can gauge a ½-inch line on the edges of the board and plane down to the line.

Jointing an Edge

The edges of a board must be straight without dips and bumps, and they must be square with the face of the board. The process of getting a rough edge square and true is called *jointing*. The jointer plane is the tool designed for edge-jointing. Its long sole ensures a straight edge.

Place the board in the vise, with its edge up. This will be the reference edge used for future measurements. Check the edge with a straightedge for high spots, and use a square to determine what needs to be done to make the edge 90 degrees to the face.

Next, use a jointer to plane the edge (Illus. 1-40). Make sure that you hold the plane square with the face of the board. If necessary, you can use shooting boards to help guide the plane, but with experience you should be able to get a square, true edge with the jointer plane alone. (See page 25 for a description of shooting boards.)

The long sole of the jointer will ride on the high spots, so at first the plane will only take a cut at the high spots. You can hear and see that the plane is cutting only in some spots along the edge of the board. The shavings will come out of the throat in short lengths. When the plane cuts evenly along the length of the board, the edge is straight. You can tell when you reach this point because the shaving will emerge from the plane in one continuous length. At this point, sight along the edge. If you have been using the proper technique, the edge should be dead straight.

A common problem when planing is to exert more downward pressure in the middle of the board, resulting in a slightly concave edge. To correct this, apply downward pressure to the heel at the beginning of the stroke and to the toe near the end of the stroke.

Illus. 1-40. Joint the edge of the board with the board clamped in the bench vise and supported by pegs on the front of the bench. The long sole of the jointer will ride on the high spots, so at first the plane will only take a cut at the high spots. When the plane cuts evenly along the length of the board, the edge is straight.

Illus. 1-41. Two boards with straight edges can be used as shooting boards to guide a plane for edge-jointing. The shooting boards are clamped on either side of the work. Use a square to make sure that the boards are aligned with each other. If they are not, the jointed edge will not be square with the face of the board. Even a short smooth plane can be used for jointing when shooting boards are used.

Shooting Boards

Even a short plane can be used for edge-jointing if you use shooting boards. These are simply boards with straight, true edges that are used to guide the plane. A simple and easy-to-use shooting board can be made from two boards with straight edges. The boards must be longer than the board to be jointed.

To use the shooting boards, place them on both sides of the work. Lightly clamp them in place and use a square to align their ends so that the two boards are even. Line up the boards with the lowest place on the edge and move them about 1/16″ lower. Now, clamp them firmly and place the whole assembly in the vise (Illus. 1-41).

Now you can plane the edge. It will be obvious where the high sections are; plane them down first. When you have worked down the high parts, plane along the entire edge in a continuous stroke. As you get close to the shooting boards, exaggerate the skew of the plane so that its toe is over one board and its heel is over the other. Stop planing when the toe and heel rub lightly all along the shooting boards.

You can make another type of shooting board for jointing an edge by cutting a rabbet along the edge of a board. The rabbet should be ¾ inch wide and ¼ inch deep. Make sure that the board you use to make the shooting board has a straight edge. It is also important that the rabbet be cut accurately. The fillister plane described in Chapter 4 can be used to make the rabbet.

To use this shooting board, place it in the vise next to the board to be jointed. Align its boards so that the shoulder of the rabbet on the one board is slightly below the edge of the other board. Make sure that the cheek of the plane is square with its sole. Place the plane on the work and press the cheek of the plane against the rabbet of the shooting board. This will keep the plane from tipping out of square. Plane the board until the sole of the plane is riding on the shoulder of the rabbet. Because there is about a ¼-inch gap between the cheek and the corner of the iron, the plane won't cut into the shooting board.

Shooting boards can also be used to shoot the end square and to shoot mitres. To make the end

Illus. 1-42. A shooting board can be used to shoot the ends of a board square. It is important that the stop is placed exactly 90 degrees to the guide ledge.

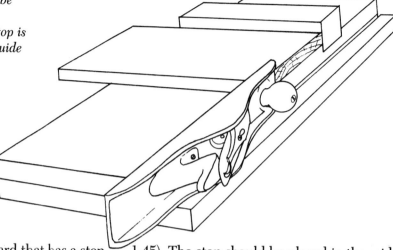

square, you need a shooting board that has a stop that is positioned exactly 90 degrees to the guide ledge in the shooting board (Illus. 1-42). Place the board against the stop and let its end overhang the ledge slightly. Place the plane on the shooting board with its cheek against the guide ledge, and plane the end of the board. Since you are planing end grain, be sure to use a sharp, well-tuned plane. As the plane passes the edge of the board, it will probably cause some splintering. You can avoid this by clamping the board firmly against the stop. The stop will then act as a backup board and prevent the splintering.

You can square the end of a board without a shooting board by using a square and a knife to mark a line and then planing to the line. Place the square against the reference edge of the board and cut a line on the face of the board with a knife (Illus. 1-43). Reposition the square to make a line on the edges; then make a line on the other face.

Next, place the board in a vise and use a bench plane to plane down to the line. This method produces a cleaner job than the shooting board, because the cut line will stop small chips and splinters from spreading past the line into the good face of the board.

Mitres can also be shot with a shooting board. There are three types of mitre joints (Illus. 1-44). Each type requires a different kind of shooting board.

To shoot a frame mitre, use a shooting board that has its stop positioned exactly 45 degrees or whatever other angle you may be using (Illus.

1-45). The stop should be placed in the middle of the shooting board and angled on both sides. The work can be placed on either side of the stop, depending on the way the mitre is cut. Place the plane on the guide ledge so that it will start cutting on the inside edge of the joint and exit past the outside edge; this will minimize splintering.

Another way to shoot mitres is with a special mitre shooting clamp. The one shown in Illus. 1-46 is designed to be clamped in a bench vise. The work is then clamped between the jaws of the clamp. The plane is guided by the 45-degree face of the clamp jaws. The E.C.E. company makes a similar clamp, which has the added capability of shooting mitre joints for an octagon (eight-sided figure). Besides the 45-degree face, the E.C.E. clamp has a face that is angled at 22.5 degrees.

Case mitres can be shot with a donkey's-ear shooting board (Illus. 1-47). This type of shooting board is particularly useful when you are working with wide mouldings. The one shown in Illus. 1-53 is designed to be used in a bench vise. The tail of the shooting board is clamped in the vise. The stop is placed in the middle of the shooting board, so that you can plane from either direction. Position the moulding with the moulded edge away from the stop, and plane towards the stop so that splintering won't occur on the moulded edge.

Edge mitres can be shot on a longer version of the donkey's-ear shooting board, with the stop placed at the end of the shooting board. When shooting long boards, use clamps to hold the work in place on the shooting board.

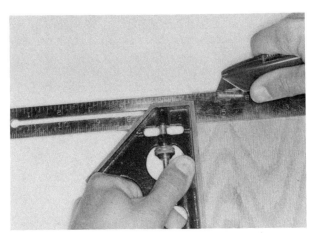

Illus. 1-43. To square the ends of a board without using a shooting board, use a square and a knife to score a line on both faces and both edges of the board. Clamp the board in a vise and plane to the lines. To avoid splintering the edges, plane into the middle from both edges.

Smoothing and Finishing

Planes produce a very smooth surface finish. Whether you buy lumber surfaced at a mill or start with rough lumber and plane it yourself, the final step is smoothing the surface with a plane. Smooth or block planes are used for finish-planing lumber surfaced at a mill. To achieve the best possible surface, you must make sure that the plane iron is sharpened correctly and the plane is tuned. See Chapters 2 and 3 for details.

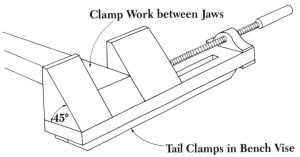

Clamp Work between Jaws

45°

Tail Clamps in Bench Vise

Illus. 1-46. A mitre shooting clamp.

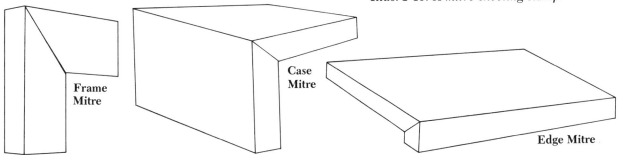

Frame Mitre

Case Mitre

Edge Mitre

Illus. 1-44. There are three types of mitre joint; each requires a different type of shooting board. The frame mitre is used on picture frames or door casing. The case mitre is used with baseboard moulding or in case construction. The edge mitre is a long joint made along the edge of a board.

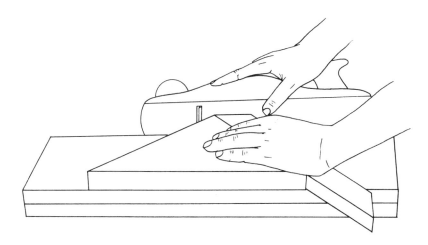

Illus. 1-45. This type of shooting board can be used to make frame mitres. The stop is positioned in the middle so that you can always place the work with its outside edge against the stop.

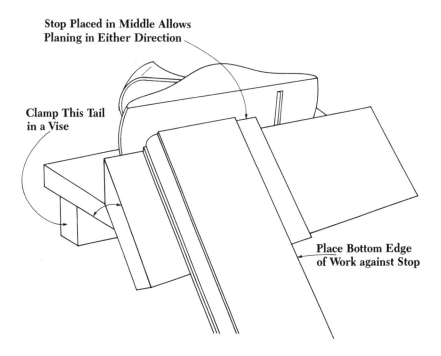

Stop Placed in Middle Allows Planing in Either Direction

Clamp This Tail in a Vise

Place Bottom Edge of Work against Stop

Illus. 1-47. The donkey's-ear shooting board is used for case mitres. When shooting the end of a moulding, place the bottom edge of the moulding against the stop so that splintering won't damage the moulded edge.

Hand planes can be very useful for surfacing large glued-up panels. Frequently, the panel will be too large to fit through the thickness planer. Hopefully, you will have glued up the panels so that there aren't many defects to correct. If this is the case, simply scrape off the glue drips with a scraper and then give the panel its final surface with a trying plane. If some of the boards are higher than others, then you can use the scrub plane and the procedure described previously to work them down before you use the jointer.

Lumber that has been surfaced with a power planer will have mill marks on its surface. Mill marks are wave-shaped marks left by the cylindrical shape of the planer head; when viewed closely, the surface of the board looks like a washboard. A planer that is well adjusted and run at the correct feed speed will leave small marks that are hardly noticeable, but a lot of commercially available lumber has large mill marks that result from a higher feed speed or a planer that is out of adjustment. A plane is the perfect tool for removing these marks. Unless the planer was severely out of adjustment, you don't have to worry about flattening the surface, so a trying plane is not necessary. A smooth plane works well in this case (Illus. 1-48). Make light, even cuts along the face of the

board with the plane skewed about 10 degrees. Overlap each previous stroke slightly. Stop as soon as all of the mill marks have been removed. You can touch up small marks left by the plane with a cabinet scraper (see Chapter 7).

A block plane can also be used for the final finishing operation. To be effective, you have to tune the plane as described in Chapter 3. Make very light cuts. Push down hard on the plane to get a shiny, slick surface.

Illus. 1-48. A smooth plane is used to give the board its final smoothing. This is a good way to remove mill marks from lumber that was surfaced with power equipment or to remove any plane marks left by the cambered edges of hand planes.

Chapter 2

SHARPENING

Keeping the plane iron sharp is one of the most important steps in maintaining your plane. The cutting edge of any tool is formed by grinding and polishing two surfaces until they meet at a sharp cutting edge. Some tools, like a knife, are bevelled on both sides to form the cutting edge. Plane irons are only bevelled on one side. The intersection between the bevel and the flat back of the iron forms the cutting edge. Both of these surfaces must be accurately ground and honed to produce a sharp cutting edge.

Disassembling the Plane

Before you can sharpen the plane iron, you must remove it from the plane. Metallic block planes are the simplest planes to disassemble. Loosen the lever cap by sliding the cam. Then pull the lever cap back until the keyhole-shaped slot can be lifted off the screw (Illus. 2-1). With the lever cap removed, simply lift out the plane iron. It is ready to be sharpened.

Metallic bench planes are slightly more complicated, but are still easy to disassemble. Lift the cam thumbpiece of the lever cap (Illus. 2-2). This will loosen the lever cap so you can pull it back to where the screw will slip through the keyhole-shaped slot. The cap iron and plane iron are attached together. You can lift this "double iron" assembly out of the throat.

Next, loosen the cap iron screw. The end of the lever cap is shaped to act as a screwdriver to fit this screw (Illus. 2-3). Once the screw is loosened about half a turn, you can slide the cap iron up the plane iron. When the end of the cap iron is about one inch above the cutting edge, twist the cap iron 90 degrees. Now, slide the cap iron all the way to the end of the slot, and the screw will slip out of the keyhole (Illus. 2-4).

Wooden transitional planes with a Bailey-type design are disassembled using the same procedure described for metallic bench planes. E.C.E. Primus planes are disassembled by first turning the adjustment screw rearwards to raise the iron up into the throat slightly. Next, loosen the tension screw nut until the cross pin of the tension screw can be moved clear of the cams on the cap iron. Pull out the cross pin and twist it 90 degrees (Illus. 2-5). You can now lift out the plane iron assembly.

There are several different techniques that can be used to disassemble a traditional wooden plane. No matter which method you use, make sure you have a hold on the plane iron so it won't drop out and get damaged.

For long planes like the jointer, hold the plane sole-up. Grasp the stock with your left hand, near the tote. Put your right hand into the throat and hold on to the wedge and iron. Next, hit the fore end of the stock on the bench. This will loosen the wedge, and you should be able to remove it.

Another way to loosen the wedge of long planes is to strike the top of the fore end of the stock with a mallet. This will loosen the wedge so it can be removed. There is often a metal striking button at this location. To keep the plane iron from falling

Illus. 2-1. *Metallic block planes are the simplest to disassemble. Loosen the lever cap by sliding the cam. Then pull the lever cap back until the keyhole-shaped slot can be lifted off the screw. With the lever cap removed, lift out the plane iron.*

Illus. 2-2. *To disassemble a metallic bench plane, lift the cam thumbpiece of the lever cap. Pull the lever cap back to where the screw will slip through the keyhole-shaped slot. Then lift the "double iron" assembly out of the throat.*

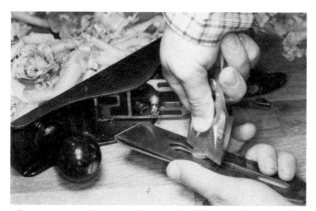

Illus. 2-3. *To disassemble the double iron, loosen the cap iron screw. The end of the lever cap is shaped to act as a screwdriver to fit this screw.*

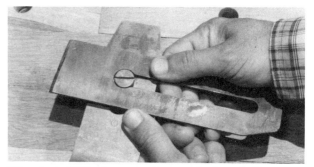

Illus. 2-4. *With the screw loosened about half a turn, slide the cap iron up the plane iron. When the end of the cap iron is about one inch above the cutting edge, twist the cap iron 90 degrees. Now, slide the cap iron all the way to the end of the slot and the screw will slip out of the keyhole.*

Illus. 2-5. *To disassemble E.C.E. Primus planes, first turn the adjustment screw rearwards to raise the iron up into the throat slightly. Next, loosen the tension screw nut until the cross pin of the tension screw can be moved clear of the cams on the cap iron. Pull out the cross pin and twist it 90 degrees. You can now lift out the plane iron assembly.*

Illus. 2-6. *One way to remove the wedge of a traditional plane is to hit the heel end of the stock down hard on the workbench. Hold the plane with your fingers on its sole and your thumb inside its throat. Press your thumb against the wedge and iron to prevent the iron from falling out.*

out, hold the stock in your left hand with your fingers on the sole and your thumb inside the throat. Press your thumb against the wedge and iron.

Horn planes and smaller planes require a different technique. The horn will be damaged if you strike it against the bench, and smaller planes will have the striking button at the heel. On these planes, remove the wedge by striking the heel with a mallet harder than you would when making adjustments. Hold the plane in your left hand with your fingers on its sole and your thumb inside its throat. Press your thumb against the wedge and iron to prevent the iron from falling out. You can also remove the wedge by hitting the heel end of the stock down hard on the workbench (Illus. 2-6).

Sharpening Stages

The sharpening process consists of three steps: grinding, honing, and stropping. In the sharpening directions in this chapter I cover the second and third steps first. Grinding is a necessary step in the sharpening process, but it is my opinion that most novices grind the cutting edge too often. When you purchase a new plane, the iron has been accurately ground at the factory. If you are careful with your planes so they don't get large nicks, you can sharpen them many times before you will need to use a grinder.

Grinding is necessary when the cutting edge needs reshaping or if it has serious damage like a large nick. However, when used incorrectly, the grinder can do more harm than good. The grinder removes metal very quickly, so it is possible that an inexperienced operator will get the iron out of square or the angle of the bevel wrong. The angle of the bevel on the iron is very important to the cutting efficiency of the iron. Beginners should keep the iron at the same angle as it comes from the factory. In Chapter 3, I describe how to change it for various reasons.

The most serious potential problem when using a grinder is overheating the iron. You must proceed slowly and dip the iron in water often to keep it cool. If the iron gets too hot, it will turn blue in a small spot. This means that the steel has lost its temper in that spot, so it will not hold a keen edge. The only solution is to grind off the affected area, but in so doing, it is possible to burn a new spot. For these reasons, do not use the grinder until you have more experience. If possible, practise on an inexpensive plane iron until you can grind it without overheating it.

Whetstones

You can achieve a sharp cutting edge by honing the plane iron on whetstones. (Whetstones are commercial stones used to sharpen edge tools.) Before you can use a new plane for the first time, you will usually have to hone it. Most planes come from the factory with the iron ground accurately, but not honed. After you have used the plane for a while, the edge will dull; honing the edge will restore its cutting efficiency.

You will need medium and fine whetstones to hone plane irons. The stones should be about 2 inches wide and 8 inches long. The traditional favorites are soft Arkansas and hard Arkansas stones. These are oilstones and must be used with oil. The oil keeps the stone from clogging up with grit and steel particles. If you don't use enough oil, the surface of the stone will become glazed and it won't cut as quickly. I prefer to use honing oil that is specially made for sharpening, but you can also use light machine oil or mineral oil.

There are also waterstones available that do a very good job. They use water instead of oil. The water serves the same purpose; it floats away the grit and steel particles to keep the face of the stone from becoming glazed. Waterstones can be placed in a shallow plastic trough that contains the water.

If you already have some high-quality whetstones, use the ones you have. If you need to buy new whetstones, I recommend that you buy ceramic whetstones (Illus. 2-7). These stones are made from man-made sapphires bonded together with a ceramic bonding agent and heated to 3,000 degrees Fahrenheit. These ceramic stones have two major advantages. First, they are so hard they will not wear appreciably on the face. Most whetstones wear as they are used. This can lead to a dished-out section in the middle of the stone.

Illus. 2-7. To achieve a sharp cutting edge, you need quality whetstones. The stones should be about 2 inches wide and 8 inches long. If you already have some high-quality whetstones, use the ones you have. However, if you have to buy new whetstones, buy ceramic whetstones.

When the face of the stone wears, it is impossible to hone a straight edge. After much use, ordinary stones must be lapped to flatten the face. Ceramic stones will remain flat even after years of use, so you are assured of an accurate cutting edge.

The second advantage in using ceramic stones is that they don't require any oil or water. Oil is particularly messy when used to sharpen woodworking tools. A little oil left on your hands can get rubbed onto the wood of the project and cause a problem later when you apply a finish.

In the directions that follow for honing the iron, ceramic stones are used. If you will be using oilstones, be sure to place a few drops of oil on the stone before each step. If you will be using waterstones, be sure to use plenty of water on the stones.

Maintaining Whetstones The whetstones must be protected when not in use. Wood dust will clog the stone, so the stones should be stored in a covered box. Ceramic stones come in a plastic box. High-quality natural stones often come in a wooden box. If you have some stones that didn't come with a storage box, make a wooden box for them.

After several uses, the face of a ceramic stone will become clogged with steel particles. To re-move the particles, hold the stone under running water and scrub it with a nylon scouring pad.

After much use, the surface of oilstones and waterstones may become glazed or uneven. To flatten the surface and remove the glaze, use a technique called *lapping.* You will need a surface that you know to be perfectly flat. A piece of thick plate glass works well. Place a piece of 180-grit silicon-carbide wet or dry sandpaper on top of the glass. Wet the sandpaper with water. Place the whetsone face-down on the sandpaper. Hold the sandpaper stationary with one hand as you rub the stone back and forth with the other. If the surface of the stone is flat but glazed, it will only take a few passes to remove the glaze. It may take a considerable amount of rubbing to flatten the face of a badly worn stone. When the face is flat, wash the stone under running water to remove all traces of the silicon carbide abrasive.

Honing the Iron

The first time you hone a plane iron, you have to hone the back. Once this is done, you won't have to do it again during the life of the iron. A new iron will have coarse scratches on its back left by the factory surface grinder. Remember that the cutting edge is formed by the intersection of the back and the bevel. If the back is not honed, then the cutting edge will only be half sharpened. It would be like only honing one side of a knife blade.

To hone the back of the iron, begin with the medium ceramic stone. Lay the iron flat on the stone, with the area that begins at the cutting edge and extends about 2 inches up the iron in contact with the stone. Press the iron down with the fingers of one hand, and hold the part of the iron that extends past the stone with your other hand (Illus. 2-8).

Now, rub the iron back and forth across the length of the stone. Occasionally check your progress by examining the back of the iron. If you can still see the grinding marks, then wipe off the stone with a dry rag and resume the honing operation. Once all of the grinding marks have been honed away on the 2-inch section of the iron, you can stop.

Next, switch to the fine stone and repeat the

procedure. Once all of the scratches left by the medium stone are gone, you can stop. From now on you can start the honing process by honing the bevel.

To hone the bevel, you must hold the iron at the proper angle. Following is a description of the process for honing the plane iron *freehand*. There are a variety of jigs sold for the purpose of holding

Illus. 2-8. The first time you hone a plane iron, you have to hone its back. Once this is done, you don't have to do it again during the life of the iron. Lay the iron flat on the stone with the area beginning at the cutting edge and extending about 2 inches up the iron in contact with the stone. Press the iron down with the fingers of one hand, and hold the part of the iron that extends past the stone with your other hand.

the iron at the correct angle. If you choose to use a jig, the process is the same except that the jig will hold the angle for you. It is good to know how to hone an iron without using any jigs, so try this technique first. If you just can't seem to hold the plane iron steady, then get one of the sharpening jigs.

The cutting edge is actually composed of two bevels at slightly different angles (Illus. 2-9). The primary bevel is the wider bevel. The secondary bevel is a very narrow band that forms the actual cutting edge. The secondary bevel is also called a *microbevel*. (Chapter 3 contains more information about microbevels.) When you buy a new plane, the primary bevel has been ground at the factory, but usually the job of honing the secondary bevel is left to you. By grinding the primary bevel to a shallower angle than the optimum honing angle, the manufacturer has made the job of honing easier for you. When you hold the iron at the correct honing angle, you are removing metal only from a narrow area at the tip of the bevel instead of trying to hone away metal across the entire face of the bevel.

The addition of a secondary bevel also allows for greater back clearance. If there is not enough back clearance on the plane iron, there will be increased friction. This makes it harder to push the plane, and it generates heat that can cause the cutting edge to dull more quickly.

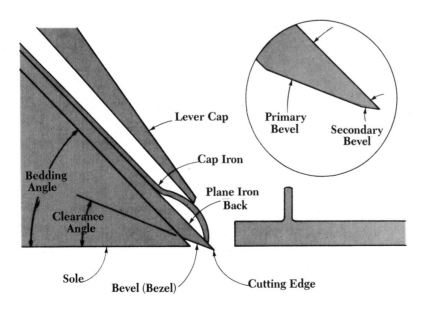

Illus. 2-9. This illustration shows the bevels on the plane iron and the associated components of a plane. The technical name for the bevel is "bezel," but most people simply call it the bevel.

Each time you hone the iron, the secondary bevel will get wider. Eventually, it will get so wide that honing becomes more difficult. When the secondary bevel gets close to ¹⁄₁₆ inch in width, it is time to regrind the primary bevel to the original grinding angle. You can extend the time between grindings by honing the primary bevel occasionally on the medium stone.

If this is the first time the cutting edge will be honed after grinding, then start with the medium ceramic stone. If the edge has been honed previously, then examine the cutting edge; if it has small nicks or it is extremely dull, begin with the medium ceramic stone. If the edge is only slightly dull but not nicked, skip this step and proceed to the fine ceramic stone. Remember that the directions given here are for ceramic stones. If you are using oilstones, the procedure is the same except that you should drip some oil on the face of the stone. If you are using waterstones, flood the stone with water.

Grip the plane iron bevel-down in your right hand with your index finger on top. Then hook your left thumb under the iron and use the rest of your left hand to press down on the iron near its cutting edge (Illus. 2-10). Holding the iron this way gives you good control, and you can exert even pressure across the iron.

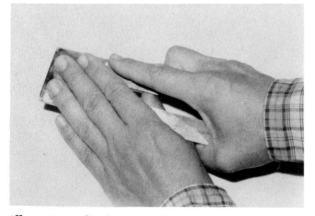

Illus. 2-10. After gripping the iron in your right hand, hook your left thumb under the iron and use the rest of your left hand to press down on the iron near the cutting edge. Holding the iron this way gives you good control, and you can exert even pressure across the iron.

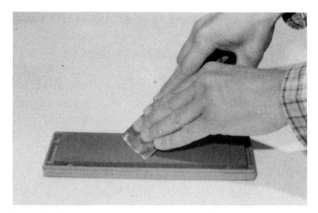

Illus. 2-11. When the iron is wider than the stone, it is necessary to hold the iron askew to get the entire cutting edge on the stone.

Begin by honing the primary bevel. The sole purpose of honing the primary bevel is to keep the secondary bevel from getting too wide. If this is the first time the plane iron has been honed after grinding, or if you prefer to grind the primary bevel when the secondary bevel gets too wide, you can skip this step and proceed directly to honing the secondary bevel.

To hone the primary bevel, place the iron on the stone, bevel-down. If the width of the iron is less than the width of the stone, hold the iron square across the stone. If the iron is wider than the stone, it is necessary to hold the iron askew to get the entire cutting edge on the stone (Illus. 2-11). Lightly rock the iron until you can feel that the primary bevel is resting flat on the face of the stone. Lock your wrists to maintain the angle. Stand with your feet apart and facing the whetstone squarely. Your knees should be flexed slightly, and your shoulders should face forward. Press down on the iron uniformly with the fingers of your left hand and the index finger of your right hand. Push the iron forward. After reaching the far end of the stone, pull the iron back to the near end. Repeat this motion several times.

Now, look at the secondary bevel. If it is too wide, make several more back-and-forth strokes, and then check the width of the secondary bevel again. Keep working until the secondary bevel is very narrow, but it is not necessary to completely remove the secondary bevel. If you should happen to completely hone away the secondary bevel, it is not a problem; just follow the procedure given below to hone a new one.

To hone the secondary bevel, grip the iron as described above and place it on the stone with the primary bevel resting flat on the face of the stone. Then rock the iron forward so that the rear of the primary bevel is slightly raised off the stone.

The usual grinding angle for the primary bevel is 25 degrees. The honing angle for the secondary bevel should be about 30 degrees. The first few times you hone, you may want to check the angle by placing a drafting triangle between the stone and the iron. This will help you determine how much forward rocking is necessary to get a 30-degree angle. With experience, you won't have to use the triangle.

Once you have the iron at its correct honing angle, lock your wrists and move the iron in a straight line back and forth along the entire length of the stone. You should be able to maintain the angle of your hands during this back-and-forth movement; however, if you feel that the angle has changed, stop and check the placement of the bevel on the stone.

The purpose of using the medium stone is to remove small nicks in the cutting edge, so stop as soon as you have removed enough of the old edge to eliminate the nicks. As you sharpen the iron, you will see a wire edge forming. A wire edge is a thin curl of steel that forms along the cutting edge. This occurs when the stone is cutting right up to the intersection between the back of the iron and the bevel. When you are removing nicks, a fairly large wire edge may form because you are removing a lot of metal. If you didn't have to remove much of the old edge, the wire edge may be so small that you won't even see it; however, you will be able to feel a small burr. To avoid cutting yourself, feel for the burr with your finger nail. Place your fingernail on the back of the iron and lightly rub it off the iron across the edge. The formation of a wire edge is an indication that you have honed the edge enough.

To remove the wire edge, use a process called *backing off*. Place the back of the iron flat on the face of the fine stone. I use the fine stone to back off the iron even when I am using the medium

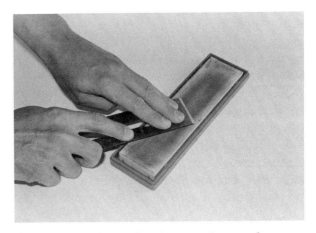

Illus. 2-12. Backing off is the procedure used to remove the wire edge that forms when the bevel is honed. Place the back of the iron flat on the face of the fine stone and rub it back and forth a few strokes. The iron must be perfectly flat on the stone. If you lift it even slightly, you will create a double bevel that will change the cutting angle.

stone on the bevel. The reason is that I have already honed the back with the fine stone, so I don't want to scratch it with the coarser medium stone.

When backing off, make sure that the iron is perfectly flat on the stone. If it is lifted even slightly, a double bevel will be created that will change the cutting angle. Rub the iron back and forth a few strokes (Illus. 2-12). Now, feel the edge again. There should be no burr on the back.

Next, use the fine stone to hone the secondary bevel. The purpose of the fine stone is to polish the surface that forms the cutting edge. Since the primary bevel does not extend to the cutting edge, it is never necessary to hone the primary bevel with the fine stone.

When using the fine stone to hone the secondary bevel, use exactly the same technique as described for the medium stone. When you can feel a small burr on the back of the cutting edge, stop and back off the iron. Usually, you will find that there is now a burr on the bevel side. Turn the iron bevel-side down and use the same technique as previously used to hone the bevel. Take two or three light strokes, and then feel for a burr. It may be necessary to back off the iron one more time to finally eliminate the burr.

Stropping

You can stop at this stage and have a very sharp cutting edge. I like to take the process one step further and strop the cutting edge. Stropping is often overlooked when plane irons are being sharpened, but it can be very effective. Stropping makes the edge sharper initially, and it can save on resharpening time. Unless the iron is nicked or seriously dulled, you can usually bring it back to a razor-sharp edge by stropping alone.

A strop is a piece of leather that is impregnated with fine abrasive. The leather strap that hangs from a barber's chair is a flexible strop used to sharpen the barber's straight razor. For plane irons, you need a rigid strop. I like to use a strop that is the same size as the whetstones.

To make a strop, cut a block of closed-grained hardwood, such as maple, the same size as your stones. Make sure that the face of the wood is perfectly flat. Glue a piece of leather to it.

Next, rub the surface of the strop with a fine abrasive. I use polishing compound. Polishing compound is a fine abrasive paste used to rub out finishes such as lacquer or varnish. You can also use jeweller's rouge or silicon carbide paste. Jeweller's rouge is a reddish polishing compound used to polish metal. Silicon carbide paste is a black paste used by machinists to smooth and polish metal parts. It comes in several grades; use the finest grade you can get. Rub the abrasive into the strop until it is well worked in. The strop is now ready to use.

Make all of the strokes by pulling the iron rearwards along the strop. If you push the iron forward, it will cut into the strop. Place the iron bevel-side down and adjust its angle until the bevel is flat against the strop. Pull the iron back until you reach the near end of the strop; then reposition it at the far end again, to make another stroke (Illus. 2-13). After two or three strokes, turn the iron over and strop the back using the same procedure as described for backing off, except that all of the strokes are made pulling the iron rearwards.

The iron now has a very sharp edge that will take extremely fine shavings off the wood. As soon as you sense that its edge is becoming dull, repeat the stropping process. You should be able to create a sharp edge by just stropping several times before you have to use the stones. If stropping won't produce the desired edge, then hone the iron on the fine stone. Unless the iron has been seriously dulled or nicked, it is not necessary to use the medium stone.

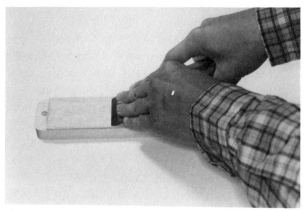

Illus. 2-13. When stropping the iron, make all of the strokes by pulling the iron rearwards. Start with the bevel flat against the strop for a few strokes; then turn the iron over and strop the back.

Illus. 2-14. To assemble a metallic bench plane, first attach the plane iron, and then place the double-iron assembly in the throat, as shown here. It should rest flat on the frog. Wiggle it around a little to get the fingers of the Y adjusting lever to line up with the cutout in the cap iron. Move the lateral adjustment lever back and forth until it is seated in the slot of the plane iron. Turn the adjustment knob until the cutting edge is just barely projecting from the mouth. Then replace the lever cap and snap down the cam thumbpiece.

Assembling the Plane

When you reassemble the plane, take care to protect the cutting edge. If you hit the edge against another metal part of the plane, you can nick it. To reassemble the *block plane*, place the iron in the throat with its bevel up. Position the iron on the bed so that its cutting edge is square in the throat and projects slightly below the sole. Wiggle the iron around until you feel the teeth of the adjusting lever fit into the slots in the iron.

Next, reinstall the lever cap. Before you tighten it, try the adjustments to make sure they are engaged properly. Then slide the cam thumbpiece to lock the lever cap in place.

The first step in assembling a *bench plane* is to attach the cap iron. Hold the cap iron at a 90-degree angle. Slip the screwhead on the cap iron through the keyhole slot in the plane iron. Slide the screw down the slot about one inch; then twist the cap iron to line up with the plane iron. Slide the cap iron down until its end is close to the cutting edge. Its exact position depends on the type of work you will be doing. For general planing, ⅟₁₆ inch away from the edge is a good distance. For fine work, it should be closer to ⅟₃₂ inch away from the edge, and for very coarse work it can be up to ⅛ inch away from the cutting edge. Use the end of the lever cap as a screwdriver to tighten the cap-iron screw.

Place the double-iron assembly in the throat. It should rest flat on the frog (Illus. 2-14). Wiggle it around slightly to align the fingers of the Y adjusting lever with the cutout in the cap iron. Move the lateral adjustment lever back and forth until it is seated in the slot of the plane iron. Turn the adjustment knob until the cutting edge is just barely projecting from the mouth.

Next, place the lever cap on top of the cap iron. Slip it down so that the screw engages in the keyhole slot. Snap down the cam. If the cam is too difficult to snap down, loosen the lever cap screw ⅛ turn. If the lever cap doesn't hold the plane iron securely, tighten the lever cap screw ⅛ turn.

To assemble the *E.C.E. Primus wooden plane*, slip the cap iron onto the plane iron. The cap iron is attached with two screws (Illus. 2-15). Before completely tightening the screws, adjust the position of the cap iron to the desired distance away from the cutting edge. Turn the cross pin of the tension screw to the vertical position.

Next, insert the plane-iron assembly into the throat of the plane (Illus. 2-16). Now, examine the end of the tension screw. You will see the word *oben* stamped on it. *Oben* is the German word for top. Twist the cross pin so that the part of the tension screw with *oben* stamped on it is on top.

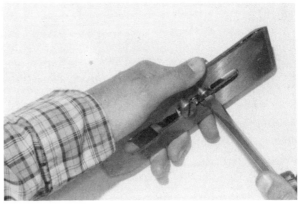

Illus. 2-15. The cap iron of the E.C.E. Primus plane is attached with two screws. Before completely tightening the screws, adjust the position of the cap iron to the desired distance away from the cutting edge.

Illus. 2-16. To install the double-iron assembly in the E.C.E. Primus plane, first turn the cross pin of the tension screw to the vertical position. Then insert the plane iron assembly into the throat of the plane. Twist the cross pin so that the part of the tension screw with oben *stamped on it is on top. Tighten the tension screw nut until the cross pin is seated between the cams on the cap iron.*

Illus. 2-17. To assemble a traditional wooden plane, hold the plane in your left hand with your fingers on the sole and your thumb inside the throat. Place the heel of the plane on the bench. With your right hand, position the iron in the throat. Press down on the iron with your left thumb to hold it in place while you put the wedge in with your right hand. Then tap the wedge in with a mallet.

Next, tighten the tension screw nut until the cross pin is seated between the cams on the cap iron. Try the adjusting screw. If it seems too hard to adjust, loosen the tension screw nut. If there is not enough tension, tighten the tension screw nut.

To assemble a *traditional wooden plane*, hold the plane in your left hand with your fingers on the sole and your thumb inside the throat. Place the heel of the plane on the bench. With your right hand, position the iron in the throat. Press down on the iron with your left thumb to hold it in place while you put the wedge in with your right hand (Illus. 2-17). Tap the wedge in with a mallet.

Now, adjust the iron setting by tapping with a mallet as described in Chapter 1. After the final adjustment, drive the wedge tight with the mallet.

Grinding

When the cutting edge of the plane iron becomes badly nicked, extremely dull, or the secondary bevel becomes too wide, it is time to grind it. Grinding can also be used to change the angle of the bevel or the camber of the edge. *Always wear safety glasses, goggles, or a face shield when you are grinding.* A shower of sparks and particles of abrasive and steel fly from the grinder. Serious injury can result if any of these get into your eyes.

There are several types of grinders that can be used to grind the plane iron. The most common type is the high-speed grinder. This grinder will remove metal quickly, but it also heats up the work quickly, so you must use extreme care not to burn the iron.

Plane irons are made from heat-treated steel. If the edge is heated too much, it can reverse the heat treatment and soften the steel. When this happens, the iron "loses its temper." The steel will change colors as it heats up. Light shades of straw color indicate that the steel is getting too hot. When it turns blue, the steel has lost its temper. The only solution is to grind away all of the blue area.

To keep from overheating the steel, you should frequently quench the iron in water. Don't wait for the steel to start changing color before you quench it. Get in the habit of quenching the iron every few seconds. A good way to gauge when to quench the steel is to watch the water drops on the back of the iron. As soon as all of the drops left from the last quenching have dried up, it is time to quench the iron again.

Professional machinists use a mist coolant system to cool steel as they grind. This is the most efficient way to prevent overheating. You can get a similar effect by spraying water from a spray bottle onto the plane iron as you grind. To be most effective, the mist should be constant. This means, that you will either have to grind with one hand or have an assistant run the sprayer as you grind.

There is a new type of grinding wheel called a *friable abrasive wheel* that does not heat up the blade as quickly as the standard type. The abrasive grains continually fracture during the grinding process. This exposes a new sharp edge, and particles that fly off carry away some of the heat.

Slow-speed grinders are designed to help prevent overheating. Slow-speed grinders can be motor-driven or hand-operated. Hand-operated

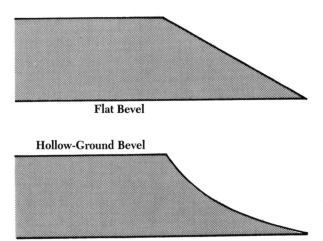

Flat Bevel

Hollow-Ground Bevel

Illus. 2-18. Using a grinding wheel produces a hollow-ground edge. A belt grinder will produce a flat bevel.

grinders require that you hold the iron with only one hand, but they give you more control over the speed.

Before using any grinding wheel to sharpen a plane iron, make sure that the face of the wheel is flat and square. Use a wheel dresser to flatten the face and expose new, sharp abrasive particles.

When you grind the cutting edge on a grinding wheel, the face of the bevel will be slightly concave. This is called a *hollow-ground edge*. Many woodworkers prefer a hollow-ground edge, while others prefer a flat bevel (Illus. 2-18). Each has advantages. The best way to determine which one to use is to try both methods and decide for yourself.

The smaller the grinding wheel, the more concave the hollow grinding will be. If the hollow grind is too deep, the edge will be weak. For this reason, don't use a grinding wheel with a diameter of less than 6 inches.

To grind a flat bevel, you need to use a belt grinder. There are several types made specifically for sharpening tools. Use a 120-grit belt. The belt grinder won't heat up the iron as fast as a grinding wheel, but you still need to dip the iron in water frequently.

The tool rests supplied with most grinders are not very well suited for grinding a plane iron. You can buy special grinding jigs to replace the tool

rest, or you can use the existing tool rest to steady your hand for freehand grinding.

To grind the iron freehand, make sure the angle of the tool rest is *close* to the correct angle. The iron should touch the front of the tool rest, but not the back (nearest the wheel). Hold the iron in your right hand, with your thumb on the back of the iron and your index finger on the front of the iron. With the grinder off, place the iron against the tool rest with its bevel down. This will put your thumb on top. Rest the primary bevel against the wheel. Adjust the angle of the iron until the bevel is flat against the wheel. The usual grinding angle is 25 degrees.

Next, slide your index finger forward until it

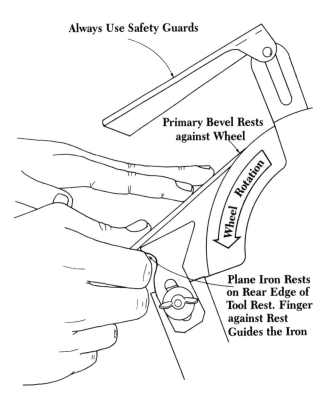

Always Use Safety Guards

Primary Bevel Rests against Wheel

Wheel Rotation

Plane Iron Rests on Rear Edge of Tool Rest. Finger against Rest Guides the Iron

Illus. 2-19. To grind the iron freehand, make sure the iron touches the front of the tool rest, but not the back. Hold the iron in your right hand with your thumb on the back and your index finger against the tool rest. Apply light pressure to the back of the iron with the fingers of your left hand. To guide the cut, keep your index finger straight across the iron and slide the iron back and forth across the tool rest.

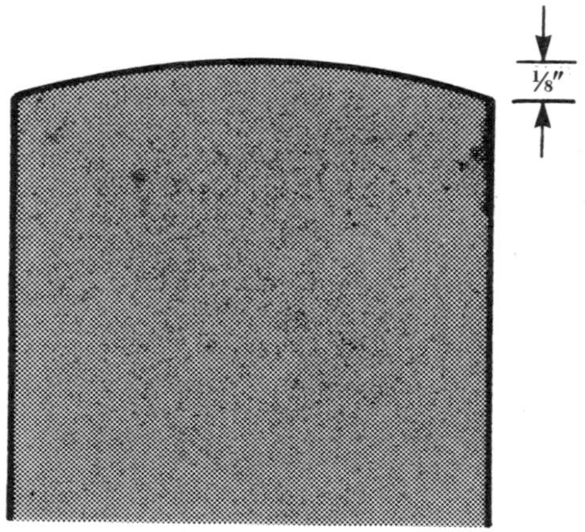

1/32"

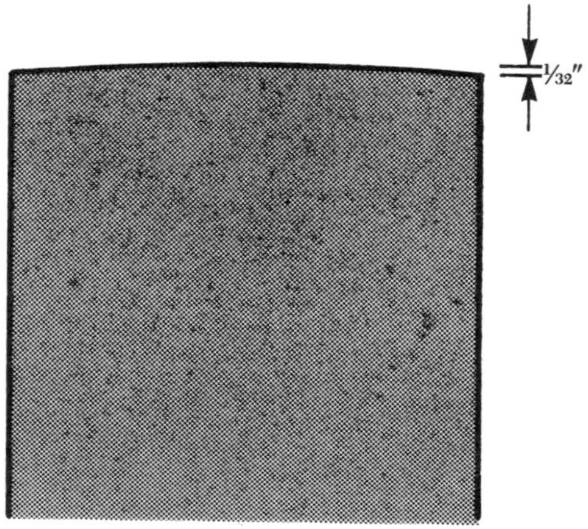

1/32" Camber: Used for General Surface Flattening After Saw Marks Have Been Removed. Usually Used on a Jack or a Fore Plane.

Flat Edge: Used for Edge-Jointing or for Finishing Work When Making a Very Fine Cut. Usually Used on a Jointer, Trying, Smooth, or Block Plane.

1/16"

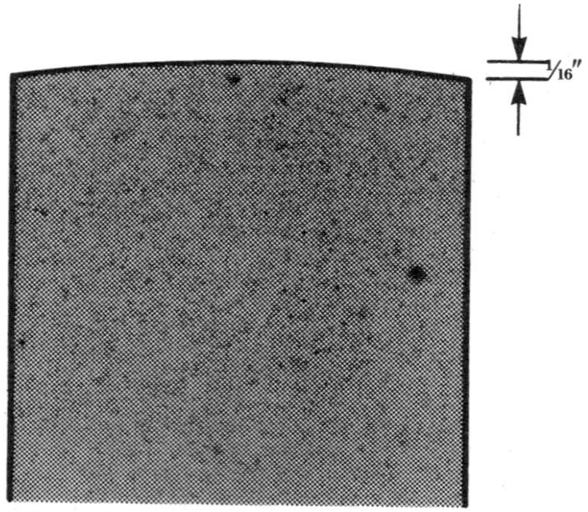

1/16" Camber: Used for Removing Saw Marks from Rough Lumber. Usually Used on a Jack or a Fore Plane.

Flat Edge with Rounded Corners: Used for Finishing Work on the Face of a Board. Rounded Corners Help Prevent Gouges. Usually Used on a Trying, Jointer, or Smooth Plane.

1/8"

1/8" Camber: Used for Hogging-Off Large Amounts of Wood. Usually Used on a Scrub or Jack Plane.

1/64"

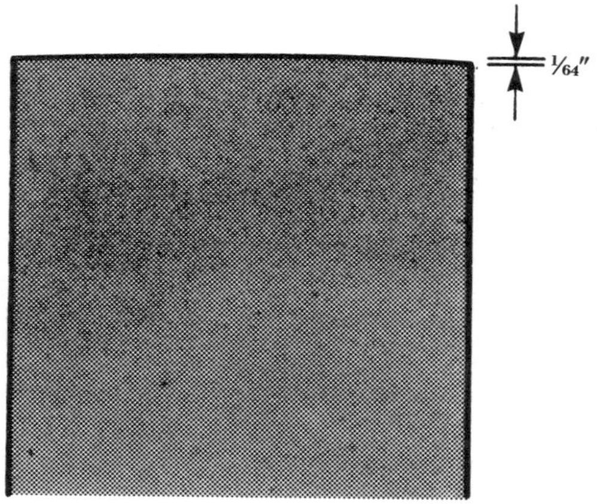

1/64" Camber: Used for Trying the Face of a Board. Usually Used on a Trying Plane or a Jointer.

Illus. 2-20. Traditionally, planes used to remove a lot of wood have cambered cutting edges. Planes used to produce a flat finished surface have straight cutting edges.

hits the front edge of the tool rest. Hold your finger in this position and remove the iron from the grinder. Turn on the grinder and position the iron. Your finger against the tool rest will guide you as you position the iron. Apply light pressure to the back of the iron with the fingers of your left hand. To guide the cut, keep your index finger straight across the iron and slide the iron back and forth across the tool rest (Illus. 2-19).

Move the iron back and forth constantly so that the bevel is ground evenly. Frequently quench the iron in water. Keep your index finger in the same position so you can quickly reposition the iron after quenching.

When a grinder is not available, you can achieve the same results using a coarse whetstone. This process is slower and requires more physical effort, but you don't have to worry about overheating the steel. For this operation, you need a fast-cutting coarse oilstone or a coarse waterstone. Ceramic stones don't cut fast enough to be used for this procedure.

When grinding with a whetstone, it is best to follow the original angle of the blade. To do this, hold the iron as described in the section on honing, and place it bevel-down on the stone. Rock the iron until you can feel that the primary bevel is resting flat on the stone. For this operation, the primary bevel should rest flat on the stone, so don't rock it forward as described in the section on honing to create a secondary bevel. Apply heavy downward pressure on the iron and rub it back and forth along the full length of the stone. Keep working until a wire edge forms on the cutting edge. Wipe the oil and grit off the plane iron, and then back it off on the fine stone. Now, switch to the medium stone and hone the secondary bevel as described earlier.

Traditionally, planes used to remove a lot of wood have a convex cutting edge, called a cambered edge. Planes used to produce a flat finished surface have straight cutting edges. Today, most planes come from the factory with a straight cutting edge. You can improve the performance of your planes if you grind the cutting edge to the camber best suited to the job it will perform.

Block planes, jointers, and smooth planes have a straight edge because they are used to produce flat surfaces and to trim joints. A cambered cutting edge is better when the plane is used to "hog" off a lot of wood. The cambers of the cutting edge can vary. Illus. 2-20 shows the various cambers used on different planes. For very rough work when a lot of waste wood must be removed, the middle of the edge can be up to ⅛ inch higher than the edges. For finer work, a flatter camber is used. A ⅟₁₆-inch camber can be used on a jack or fore plane used to remove rough saw marks from lumber. A ⅟₃₂-inch camber is good for a jack or fore plane used for general work. For trying (flattening the face of a board), use a ⅟₆₄-inch camber. For the finest work, the edge is perfectly straight. A jointer or smooth plane usually has a straight cutting edge. Even on a straight edge, it is a good idea to slightly round the corners, to prevent gouging the wood with a sharp corner.

When you have a limited number of planes, you can increase their usefulness by buying an extra iron. Grind a cambered edge on one iron, and a straight edge on the other. Now you can change the plane iron to suit the job.

Before starting the grinding, make a layout line on the back of the iron. To make the line visible, use machinist layout dye or make a line about ¼ inch wide with a permanent ink marker. Then use

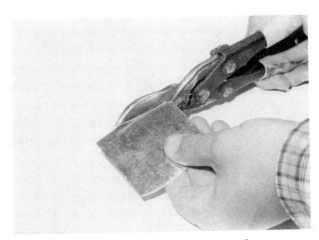

Illus. 2-21. To lay out cambered edges, make a template from thin sheet metal. Cut out the arc with tin snips, and then smooth the edge with a file. Fold up one edge in the vise to act as a positioning fence.

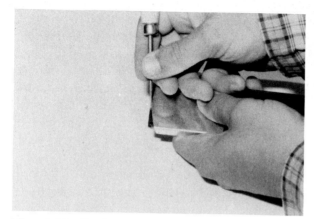

Illus. 2-22. The fence will hold the sheet-metal template square with the edge of the iron. Position the template on the back of the iron and scratch a line with a scratch awl.

a scratch awl to draw the layout line. The cutting edge should be square with the side of the iron. For irons with a straight edge, use a square to guide the awl as you scratch the line.

To lay out the cambered edges, make a template from thin sheet metal (Illus. 2-21). Cut out the arc with tin snips, and then smooth the edge with a file. Fold up one edge in the vise to act as a positioning fence. This fence should hold the template square with the edge of the iron. Position the template on the back of the iron and scratch a line with a scratch awl (Illus. 2-22).

To guide the grinding of a cambered edge, follow the directions given previously for free-hand grinding, but place your index finger so that its knuckle is in the center of the iron and just touch the tool rest with the knuckle. Rock the iron from side to side, pivoting on your knuckle. Grind the camber until it conforms to the layout line.

Rounding the corners of a plane iron will help prevent gouges caused by a sharp corner on the iron. To round the corner, press the corner against the wheel lightly and rock it back and forth a few times. Don't round too much. When you are done, the rounded corner should be hardly noticeable.

After grinding, refer to the directions given earlier in this chapter for honing.

Chapter 3

TUNING

Whether you've just bought a new plane or picked up a used one at the flea market, it will usually have to be tuned. Tuning is the process of adjusting all of the working parts to their optimum positions and removing any imperfections in the castings left from the manufacturing process. A well-tuned plane is easy to adjust and use. You can make a shaving as thin as onion skin when the plane is properly tuned.

Below I describe the tuning procedures for the parts of an old block plane I got at a flea market (Illus. 3-1). The same basic steps apply to other types of planes.

The force needed for a blade to sever the wood fibres is only a fraction of the total force needed to push a plane. The rest of the force is used to overcome drag. Drag is the accumulation of the friction generated by all parts of the plane. The sole of the plane is responsible for much drag. Lessening sole drag is one step in tuning a plane.

Adjusting the angles of the cutting edge is another step in tuning. This can help reduce the drag produced by the blade itself. The angles that are found on a standard plane iron are a compromise that gives the best all-around performance. If you want to customize a plane for a particular job, you can change the angles on its iron.

Backlash

Backlash is the slack or play in the adjustment mechanism of the plane. Sometimes backlash makes it harder to make fine adjustments to the cutting depth. On bench planes that use the standard Bailey adjustment mechanism, you can decrease the backlash by bending the Y adjusting lever. Don't attempt this modification if the plane has a cast Y adjusting lever. It can only be done on planes that have steel levers. Bend one side forward and the other back until they are each touching one side of the groove in the adjusting nut (Illus. 3-2).

Block planes that have the adjusting knob at the rear of the plane usually don't have much backlash. Block planes that use a vertical screw adjustment, such as the block plane shown in this chapter, can be tightened by removing the adjusting nut and squeezing the fingers of the adjusting lever together with pliers (Illus. 3-3).

Cap Iron

The cap iron must rest flat on the back of the plane iron with no gaps. Even a small gap can cause the plane to choke. Choking is when the throat of the plane clogs up with shavings. If a shaving can get wedged between the cap iron and the plane iron, it will crumble and clog the throat (Illus. 3-4).

If the cap iron doesn't sit on the plane iron correctly, file the cap iron to fit flat against the plane iron. To make sure that chips can't become wedged between the cap iron and the plane iron, you can slightly bevel the rear edge of the cap iron. After getting it to the right shape with a file, hone it flat on a whetstone (Illus. 3-5).

Illus. 3-1. In this chapter I describe how to tune an old block plane like the one shown here. Tuning is the process of adjusting all of the working parts to their optimum positions and removing any imperfections in the castings left from the manufacturing process.

Illus. 3-2. Backlash is the slack or play in the adjustment mechanism of the plane. You can decrease backlash on bench planes that use the standard Bailey adjustment mechanism by bending the Y adjusting lever. Bend one side forward and the other back until they are each touching one side of the groove in the adjusting nut. Don't attempt this modification if the plane has a cast Y adjusting lever.

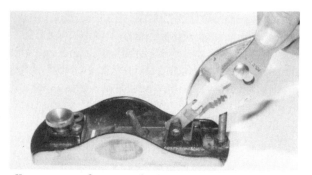

Illus. 3-3. To decrease the backlash in block planes that use a vertical screw adjustment, such as the block plane shown in this chapter, remove the adjusting nut and squeeze the fingers of the adjusting lever together with pliers.

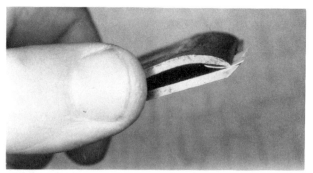

Illus. 3-4. The cap iron must rest flat on the back of the plane iron with no gaps. If the shaving gets wedged between the cap iron and the plane iron, it will crumble and clog the throat. Here you can see a shaving that has been wedged between the cap iron and the plane iron.

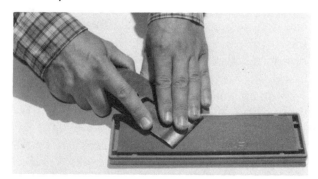

Illus. 3-5. Honing the cap iron can remove irregularities so that the cap iron will seat on the plane iron correctly. If the angle at the end of the cap iron is incorrect, it may be necessary to file it to fit flat against the plane iron. The edge of the cap iron can be slightly bevelled to the rear. After shaping it properly with a file, hone it flat on a whetstone.

Illus. 3-6. If a plane chatters even when set fine, the iron is probably not bedded correctly. Use a fine file to remove any irregularities on the bed.

Polish the top of the cap iron to make the shavings slide off easily. You can use fine steel wool or a motorized buffing wheel to do the polishing. You can also polish the cap iron by rubbing it on a leather strop that is charged with polishing compound.

Adjust the cap iron so that it is about ¹⁄₁₆ inch away from the edge for average work. For fine cuts, you can move it as close as ¹⁄₃₂ inch.

Bedding the Iron

If a plane chatters even when set fine, the iron is probably not bedded correctly. The plane iron must be fully supported by the frog or bed to prevent chattering. Disassemble the plane and look at the frog or bed. If you notice any high spots, they should be removed. For a metallic plane, use a fine file to remove the high spots. For a wooden plane, pare down the high spots with a sharp chisel. The block plane used in this chapter has no frog. The iron rests on the bed of the plane. I have filed the bed until the blade is evenly bedded (Illus. 3-6).

Adjusting the Mouth

The mouth of the plane plays an important role in preventing tear-out. The toe of the plane presses down on the wood, keeping the split started by the plane iron from progressing deeper into the wood. The only unsupported area is inside the mouth. For fine work, the mouth opening in front of the iron should be as small as possible. On the other hand, when you are hogging off a lot of wood during the roughing stages, tear-out is not as critical, but choking is a problem. In this case, the plane should have a wide throat, to keep it from choking. Opening up the mouth and throat will prevent the shavings from getting clogged.

The mouth on the block plane shown and described in this chapter is easy to adjust. Loosen the finger rest knob and slide the eccentric lever until the mouth is set to the correct opening; then retighten the knob (Illus. 3-7).

Metallic bench planes have an adjustable frog.

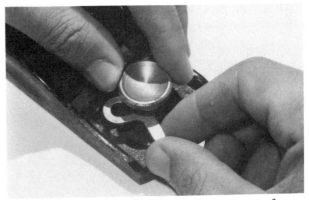

Illus. 3-7. For fine work, the mouth opening in front of the iron should be as small as possible. The mouth on the block plane shown and described in this chapter is easy to adjust. Loosen the finger rest knob and slide the eccentric lever until the mouth is set to the correct opening; then retighten the knob.

Illus. 3-8. Metallic bench planes have an adjustable frog. Moving the frog forward closes the mouth. The first step in adjusting the frog is to loosen the two screws that attach the frog to the stock.

Illus. 3-9. Better-quality metallic bench planes will have a captive screw at the rear of the frog to adjust the frog position. This is the most accurate type of frog adjustment. Turning the screw will move the frog forward or rearwards.

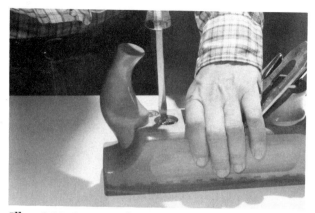

Illus. 3-10. Some modern wooden planes have an adjustable mouth. To change the mouth size, first loosen the screw on the top of the stock.

Illus. 3-11. After loosening the screw on the top of the stock of a wooden plane with an adjustable mouth, slide the adjustable section of the toe to the desired position. Hold the toe in place as you re-tighten the screw.

Illus. 3-12. To resurface the sole of a wooden plane, you need another longer plane. Place the plane that will do the cutting sole-up in a vise. Hold the plane that needs flattening just like you are going to use it to plane a board. Place it on the sole of the other plane and make a very fine cut.

Moving the frog forward closes the mouth. To adjust the frog, remove the lever cap and lift out the double iron. You will see two screws that attach the frog to the stock. Loosen these screws slightly (Illus. 3-8).

Now, look at the rear of the frog. Some metallic bench planes have a captive screw that will adjust the position of the frog. This is the most accurate type of frog adjustment. Turn this screw and the frog will slide forward or rearwards (Illus. 3-9). If your plane doesn't have this adjusting screw, just slide the frog back and forth after you have loosened the attaching screws.

You can only move the frog back so far before the back of the mouth begins to interfere with the iron. If you move the frog back farther than this, the iron will not lie flat on the frog. This will lead to chattering, and it will be difficult to adjust the depth of cut. I have seen planes come from the factory with the frog adjusted too far back, so if a new plane seems hard to adjust or has a chattering problem, check the frog adjustment.

Some modern wooden planes have an adjustable mouth. To change the mouth size, first loosen the screw on the top of the stock (Illus. 3-10). Now, slide the adjustable section of the toe to the desired position (Illus. 3-11). Hold the toe in place as you retighten the screw.

The Sole

The sole of the plane plays an important role in how well the plane cuts and how hard it is to push. A rough sole will drag on the wood, making it harder to push the plane. If the sole is not perfectly flat, the plane will not cut correctly. The toe area of the sole is particularly important, because it must press down on the wood evenly to help prevent tear-out.

The soles of wooden planes wear faster than iron soles, but they are easier to resurface. Modern wooden planes that have lignum vitae soles will last a long time before they need resurfacing, but a used plane with a softer sole is likely to need attention.

If the sole of a wooden plane is worn unevenly, you can flatten it with another plane. Pull the iron up so that its edge is about ¼ inch inside the throat. Tighten the wedge or adjusting mechanism. This will stress the sole properly. Ideally, the plane you use to resurface the sole should be longer than the one you are working on. Place the plane that will do the cutting sole-up in a vise. Hold the plane that needs flattening just like you are going to use it to plane a board. Place it on the sole of the other plane and make a very fine cut (Illus. 3-12). Stop as soon as the plane is taking an even bite all along the sole.

To flatten and polish an iron sole, you use a process called *lapping*. It is sometimes necessary to lap a new plane if it was not milled accurately at the factory. You will need a perfectly flat surface to work on. A cast-iron saw table works well. Tape a piece of 180-grit silicon carbide sandpaper to the table. One sheet is enough for the block plane shown in this chapter; you may have to tape several sheets in a row for longer planes. The plane should be totally assembled for lapping, so that its sole will be properly stressed. Adjust the iron so that its edge is inside the throat.

Wet the sandpaper with water. Place the plane flat on the sandpaper and rub it back and forth (Illus. 3-13). After a few strokes, look at the sole.

You will be able to see the high spots because they will be the only areas that have been sanded. Keep rubbing the plane until all of the high spots have been removed and the sole has an even sheen.

You can stop at this point, or you can use progressively finer grades of sandpaper to polish the sole. You can give the sole a final polish with a buffing wheel charged with polishing compound.

Plane-Iron Angles

I have found that the sharpening procedure described in Chapter 2 will consistently produce good results for virtually all uses, but in special circumstances it can be beneficial to change the cutting angle.

There are several angles involved in sharpening a plane iron. The first angle is set by the plane manufacturer and cannot be changed. It is the *bedding angle*. All other angles are determined by the way the blade is sharpened (Illus. 3-14).

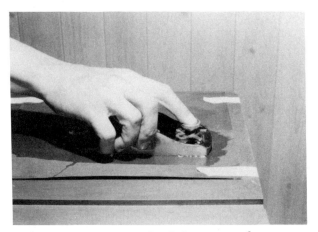

Illus. 3-13. To flatten and polish an iron sole, use a process called lapping. You need a perfectly flat work surface like a cast-iron saw table. Tape a piece of 180-grit silicon carbide sandpaper to the table. Wet the sandpaper with water. Place the plane flat on the sandpaper and rub it back and forth until all of the high spots have been removed and the sole has an even sheen.

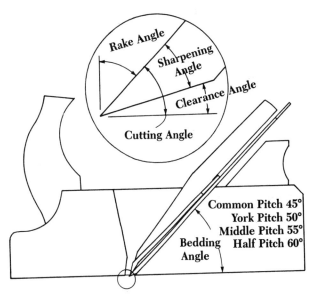

Illus. 3-14. The cutting action of a plane is determined by the interaction of the various blade or iron angles, as shown in this illustration. You can customize your plane for a particular job by changing one or more of these angles.

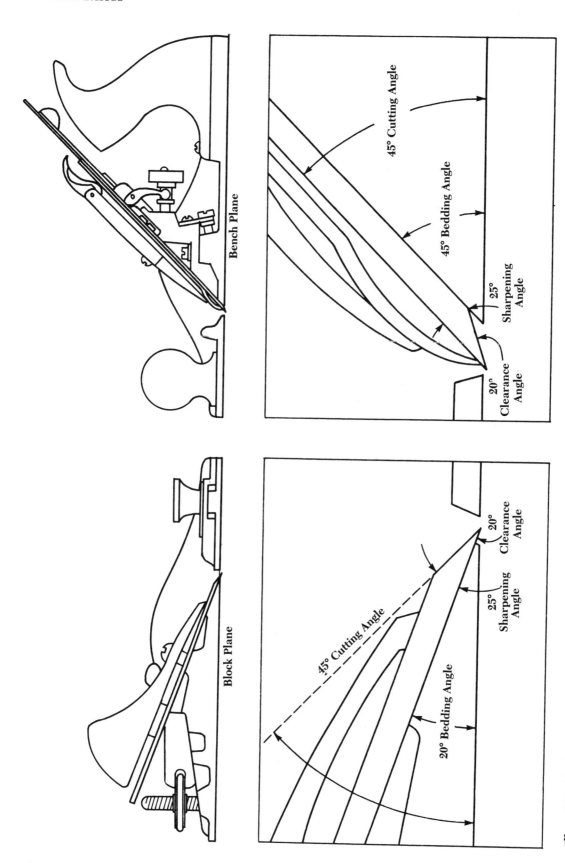

Illus. 3-15. *In this comparison of a block plane and a bench plane, you can see that changing the sharpening angle of a bench plane will not change its cutting angle, but the cutting angle of the block plane can be changed. This is one reason why a block plane is a good plane to tune up for use as a finishing plane.*

Block Plane

Bench Plane

45° Cutting Angle

45° Bedding Angle

25°
Sharpening
Angle

20°
Clearance
Angle

45° Cutting Angle

20° Bedding Angle

25°
Sharpening
Angle

20°
Clearance
Angle

The bedding angle is the angle at which the frog or bed holds the plane iron. Different types of planes have various bedding angles. Most bench planes have a bedding angle of 45 degrees. This is called *common pitch*. A lower angle makes the plane cut more easily, but it also increases the probability that the wood will tear out ahead of the iron, leaving a rough chipped surface. A higher angle makes the plane harder to push, but leaves a smoother cut. Common pitch is a compromise angle that gives a satisfactory cut with a moderate amount of pressure.

Hardwoods will be planed smoother if a plane with *York pitch* is used. York pitch is a bedding angle of 50 degrees. Some wooden planes are available with York pitch. Burl wood and other highly figured wood can be planed with less tear-out if an even higher bedding angle is used. *Middle pitch* is 55 degrees, and *half pitch* is 60 degrees. Moulding planes often use half pitch. A metallic block plane usually has a bedding angle of 12 or 20 degrees. Wooden block planes often use York pitch.

The *sharpening angle* is the most obvious angle. It's the angle that you hold the blade at while you hone it on a whetstone. The *rake angle* is determined by the bedding angle in bench planes, but in planes like the block plane, where the blade is mounted bevel-up, the rake angle is dependent on the combination of the bedding angle and the sharpening angle. The *cutting angle* is the angle formed between the work and the top of the blade. Note that in bench planes with blades mounted bevel-down, this angle is determined by the bedding angle, and cannot be changed. In planes with blades mounted bevel-up the cutting angle can be changed by varying the sharpening angle. The cutting angle is different from the sharpening angle, because the bedding angle is combined with the sharpening angle.

The *clearance angle* is the angle between the work and the bottom of the blade. In most cases, it is the clearance angle that plays the most important role in how much drag the blade has. A large clearance angle reduces drag, making the plane cut more easily; but if the clearance angle is too large, the cutting edge becomes too fragile and it

will dull quickly. When the clearance angle is too small, the blade drags on the wood. This makes it harder to push the plane and causes the blade to dull quickly. As a blade dulls, the clearance angle decreases. Eventually the cutting edge cannot come in contact with the wood, and the blade ceases to cut; this is called a *negative clearance angle*.

The blade can actually have two clearance angles. The more important angle is the clearance angle directly behind the cutting edge. If this area dulls to a negative clearance angle, the blade will not cut properly no matter how much clearance there is on the rest of the blade. The other clearance angle is formed by the remainder of the bevel. Although not as important as the clearance directly behind the cutting edge, it still helps to reduce drag if this clearance angle can be increased. This can be achieved with a technique called *microbevelling*. Microbevelling is a technique that will help to increase the clearance angle without resulting in a fragile cutting edge.

Novices should leave the geometry of the plane iron the way it was supplied from the factory and just sharpen the blade following the directions given in Chapter 2. When he is adept at the sharpening process and wants to experiment with other angles, he can use the following information.

Changing the Angle

You can customize the angle of the blade to suit your needs. The factory angles are a compromise that allows the same angle to be used for a variety of situations. Grinding the bevel to a new angle will change the cutting angle of block planes, but it will only change the clearance angle of bench planes. Illus. 3-15 shows a cross-section comparison of a block plane and bench plane. Note that as supplied from the factory, the cutting angle is the same even though the bedding angle is very different. But from this illustration you can see that changing the sharpening angle on the block plane will change the cutting angle, while the cutting angle of the bench plane will remain the same no matter what sharpening angle is used.

A good average angle is 30 degrees. You can

change the angle to anywhere in the range from 25 to 35 degrees. Soft woods can be cut better if the cutting angle is lower. Highly figured woods can chip if the cutting angle is low, so a higher angle produces better results.

Once you start changing cutting angles, you are starting on a long process of experimentation to find the angle that suits you and the jobs you are doing. It is a good idea to make a wooden angle jig or use one of the commercial blade holders when trying new angles, so that you can be sure you are sharpening the blade to the intended angle accurately.

Microbevels

I touched on the subject of microbevels in Chapter 2. In this chapter, I explain how microbevels can be used for other angles.

Microbevels are small secondary bevels at the tip of the plane iron. There is an optimum sharpening angle for each cutting situation. This angle is the same whether you are using a flat bevel, a hollow-ground bevel, or a microbevel. Only the section of the blade that is directly behind the cutting edge needs to be sharpened to this angle. If the rest of the bevel is ground to a steeper angle, then the effective clearance angle will be increased (Illus. 3-16).

There are two advantages gained by using microbevels. First, the blade will be easier to sharpen, because instead of honing off metal from the entire bevel, only a small amount of metal is removed from the tip of the blade. Second, the clearance angle is increased, reducing the pressure needed to push the plane iron through the wood.

If you want to experiment with different sharpening angles, it will be easier if you use microbevels. You can grind the bevel slightly less than the smallest angle you plan on using. Then hone the microbevel to the experimental angle. To change angles, just rehone the microbevel at the new angle. Since the microbevel is not very wide, it won't take much work to change the angle.

Following the directions given in Chapter 2 produces a microbevel of 30 degrees. Changing to another angle is a simple procedure. For example, if you want your plane to cut hard woods better, you can use a 35-degree microbevel. Begin by grinding the primary bevel to its clearance angle. In this example, I'll use 25 degrees for the primary bevel.

Next, hone the secondary bevel on the whetstone, holding the blade at the honing angle of 35 degrees. Proceed with the honing as described in Chapter 2. If you examine the blade, you will

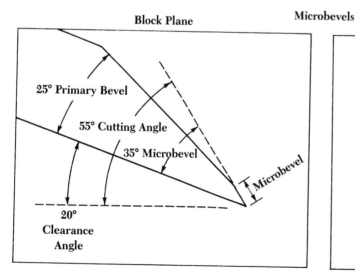

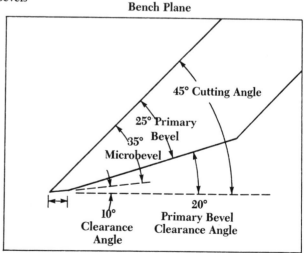

Illus. 3-16. A microbevel is a small secondary bevel at the tip of the plane iron. Changing the microbevel angle on a bench plane will change the clearance angle. Changing the microbevel on a block plane will change the cutting angle.

notice a narrow band behind the cutting edge that has been sharpened to 35 degrees; this is the microbevel. The remainder of the bevel is still ground to 25 degrees.

Changing the microbevel on a bench plane can alter the cutting characteristics to a small extent, but changing the microbevel on a block plane can have dramatic effects. This is because changing the microbevel on a bench plane won't alter the cutting angle; it only changes the clearance angle. Changing the microbevel on a block plane will change the cutting angle. This can have the same effect as switching to a plane with a different pitch. This is one of the reasons why I use a block plane to finish-plane. For example, when you are planing hard wood, a plane with York pitch will do a better job.

You can change the cutting angle of a block plane to equal the cutting angle of York pitch by simply rehoning the microbevel to a new angle. If you are planing a difficult piece of curly maple, you may need to use middle pitch or half pitch. With a block plane, all you need to do to get the same effect is to change the microbevel angle.

Table 3-1 shows the effective cutting angle produced by various microbevel angles. It contains two columns of microbevel angles, because block planes can have either a 20-degree bedding angle or a 12-degree bedding angle. Use the column that is appropriate for your plane.

Following the procedures described in this chapter, I've tuned up my old block plane so that it makes a good finishing plane (Illus. 3-17). I use it to give the wood a final finished surface. The cut is set very fine. The mouth is closed down close to the cutting edge, to prevent tear-out. The lapped sole also helps to prevent tear-out, and because it has been polished it is easy to push.

TABLE 3-1
Microbevel Angle

Cutting Angle	12-Degree Bedding Angle	20-Degree Bedding Angle
45°	33°	25°
50°	38°	30°
55°	43°	35°
60°	48°	40°

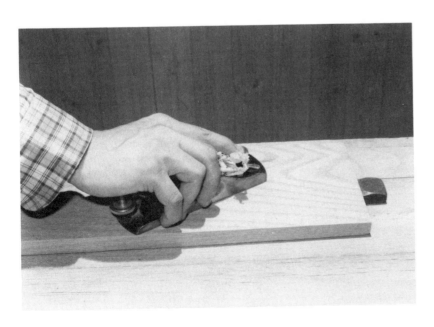

Illus. 3-17. *After a complete tuning, the old block plane makes a good finishing plane. When set for a very fine cut, it can be used to remove marks left by other planes. It will produce a shiny smooth surface that can't be equalled with sandpaper.*

Chapter 4

RABBET, PLOW, AND DADO PLANES

Rabbets, dadoes, and grooves are some of the most basic joints in woodworking (Illus. 4-1). Special types of planes are used to cut these joints. A rabbet is a step on the edge of the board; it can run with the grain or across the grain. A typical use for a rabbet that runs with the grain is to make a recess at the rear of a cabinet to accept the back. A cross-grain rabbet is typically used between the top of a cabinet and the sides.

A groove runs with the grain, and a dado runs across the grain. A groove is often used to allow for wood movement. Wood shrinks and swells with changes in humidity. If a large panel is attached rigidly to a frame, it can split as the wood shrinks. When the plane is set in a groove, the wood is held in place, but is free to shrink and swell. Dadoes are often used to attach shelves to the sides of a cabinet.

In this chapter, I discuss methods for using several types of specialized planes that are designed to make rabbets, dadoes, or grooves. These same joints can also be made using the universal combination planes described in Chapter 6.

Using Rabbet Planes

A rabbet plane has a plane iron that extends to the edge of the sole. The traditional wooden rabbet plane has remained basically the same for centuries, and it is still popular today (Illus. 4-2). A variety of different rabbet planes are available in both wooden and metallic types.

Some rabbet planes have a skewed iron. This means that the iron is set at an angle (Illus. 4-3). In Chapter 1, I describe how to hold a plane skewed. If you have tried this, you know that the plane cuts better with the iron at an angle to the forward motion of the plane. Since the rabbet plane can't be held skewed, the plane iron of some models is bedded at an angle, to achieve the same effect.

A skewed iron is most important when a plane is cutting across the grain. A straight iron will hit the wood fibres broadside and tear them out, while a skewed iron will slice the fibres, leaving a smooth surface.

A *shoulder rabbet plane* has a plane iron bedded at the low cutting angle of a block plane (Illus. 4-4). It is very useful for trimming tenon shoulders. A bullnose plane has a plane iron bedded close to the toe. This enables it to plane into tight places and make stopped joints. (A stopped joint is used to hide the joint.) The bullnose plane (Illus. 4-5) has a removable toe, allowing it to be used also as a chisel plane.

A *bench rabbet plane* resembles a jack plane, and it is sometimes called a jack rabbet (Illus. 4-6). It is used when you need to make a very wide cut.

If a rabbet plane has a fence and depth stop, it is called a *fillister*. Both wooden and metallic fillisters are still available. The cast-iron fillister plane shown in Illus. 4-7 is a good choice for a variety of

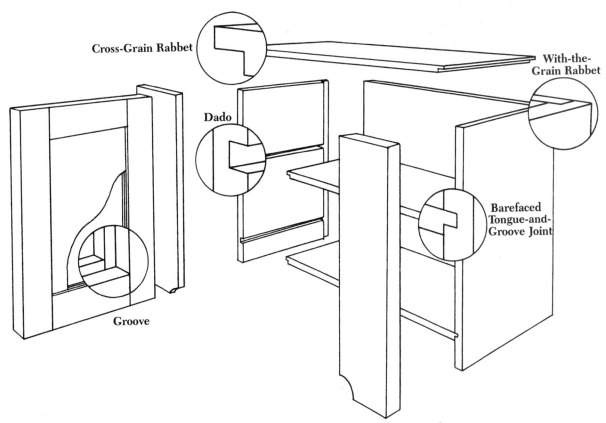

Illus. 4-1. *Rabbets, dadoes, and grooves are some of the most basic joints in wood-working. Special types of planes are used to cut these joints. This illustration shows how rabbets, dadoes, and grooves are used in the construction of a simple cabinet. The rabbet joint is used to join the top to the sides and the back to the carcass. The barefaced tongue-and-groove joint is actually a dado cut in the side of the cabinet combined with a rabbet cut on the end of the shelf. The panel of the door fits in a groove cut in the stiles and rails of the door frame.*

Illus. 4-2. *The traditional wooden rabbet plane has remained basically the same for centuries, and it is still popular today. A rabbet plane has a plane iron that extends to the edge of the sole.*

Illus. 4-3. *Some rabbet planes have a skewed iron. This means that the iron is set at an angle. The skewed iron is most important when a plane is cutting across the grain. A straight iron will hit the wood fibres broadside and tear them out, while a skewed iron will slice the fibres, leaving a smooth surface.*

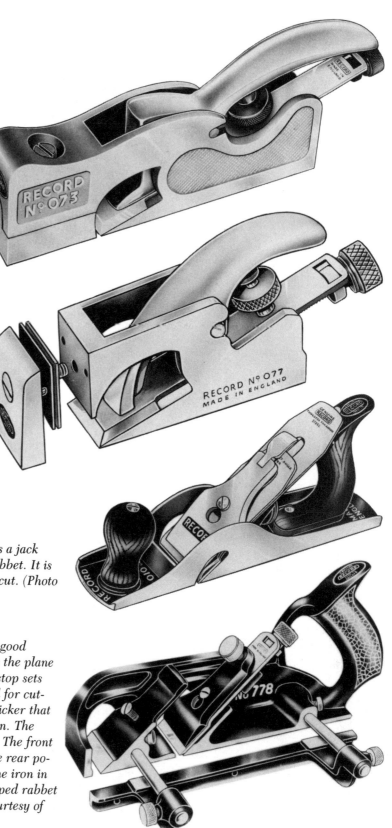

Illus. 4-4. *A shoulder rabbet plane has a plane iron bedded at the low cutting angle of a block plane. It is very useful for trimming tenon shoulders. (Photo courtesy of Record Tools.)*

Illus. 4-5. *A bullnose plane has a plane iron bedded close to the toe. This enables it to plane into tight places and make stopped joints. This bullnose plane has a removable toe. The size of the mouth can be changed by adding or removing shims. With the toe removed, the plane can be used as a chisel plane. A chisel plane has no toe, so it doesn't cut as cleanly as other planes; but it can work right into a tight corner. (Photo courtesy of Record Tools.)*

Illus. 4-6. *A bench rabbet plane resembles a jack plane, and it is sometimes called a jack rabbet. It is used when you need to make a very wide cut. (Photo courtesy of Record Tools.)*

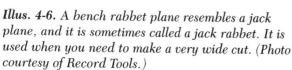

Illus. 4-7. *This cast-iron fillister plane is a good choice for a variety of jobs. A fence guides the plane and sets the width of the rabbet. A depth stop sets the depth of the cut. This plane works well for cutting cross-grain rabbets because it has a nicker that cuts the wood fibres ahead of the plane iron. The plane iron can be bedded in two positions. The front position is called the bullnose position. The rear position is the normal position. With the plane iron in the bullnose position, you can make a stopped rabbet or work close to an obstruction. (Photo courtesy of Record Tools.)*

jobs. The plane iron can be bedded in two positions. The front position is called the bullnose position. When the iron is bedded in the rear, it is in its normal position. With the plane iron in the bullnose position, you can make a stopped rabbet or work close to an obstruction. The fence guides the plane and sets the width of the rabbet. The depth stop sets the depth of the cut. For cutting cross-grain rabbets, this plane has a spur that cuts the wood fibres ahead of the plane iron. The spur is often called a nicker (Illus. 4-8).

Cutting a Rabbet with the Grain

A rabbet that runs with the grain is the simplest type of rabbet to make. You can use either a rabbet plane or a fillister.

To make the cut with a simple rabbet plane, gauge lines on the work to indicate the desired width and depth. Hold the plane in your right hand and wrap your left hand around the plane so that your fingertips are under the sole. Place the plane on the work and adjust its position to get the desired width of cut. Now, press your fingertips against the edge of the board. They will act as a fence to guide the plane (Illus. 4-9). You can also clamp or temporarily nail a board to the work to act as a fence.

To use a fillister, set the fence for the desired width and set the depth stop for the desired depth (Illus. 4-10). Turn the nicker up. The nicker is not needed to make a rabbet with the grain, and if you leave it down it can make the plane wander, because the nicker will tend to follow the grain.

Adjust the iron to remove a fairly thick shaving, but not so thick that it makes it hard to push or tears up the work. The wooden rabbet plane is adjusted in the same manner as described in Chapter 1. Hit the heel end with a mallet to raise the plane iron. To lower the plane iron, tap down on the end of the iron or hit the toe end of the plane. Tap down the wedge after each adjustment.

Metallic fillisters use several types of adjustment mechanisms. Some have a lead screw type of adjustment, and others use a lever. Usually, you must first loosen a thumbscrew on the cap iron before you make the adjustment, and tighten it

Illus. 4-8. A fillister plane has a sharp spur called a nicker that is used when making cross-grain rabbets. The nicker cuts the wood fibres ahead of the plane iron so the fibres won't tear out past the shoulder of the cut. The nicker shown here can be rotated to four positions. In one position, there is no spur. This position is used for making rabbets with the grain. Usually, only one of the three spurs is sharpened. When it becomes too short from repeated sharpenings, one of the other spurs can be used.

Illus. 4-9. To make a rabbet with the grain using a simple rabbet plane, first gauge lines on the work to indicate the desired width and depth. Then hold the plane in your right hand and wrap your left hand around the plane so that your fingertips are under the sole. Align the plane with the shoulder line and press your fingertips against the edge of the board. They will act as a fence to guide the plane.

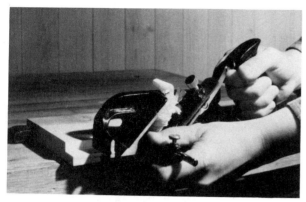

Illus. 4-10. To cut a rabbet with the grain using a fillister, set the fence for the desired width and set the depth stop for the desired depth. Turn the nicker up. The nicker is not needed to make a rabbet with the grain.

Illus. 4-11. To cut a cross-grain rabbet with a fillister, use the nicker. The first step is to score the shoulder line by placing the plane at the toe end of the board and pulling it rearwards across the face of the board.

after the adjustment is complete. When the plane iron is placed in the bullnose position, there may not be any mechanical adjustment. You must position the iron with your fingers and then tighten the thumbscrew.

If the board is about four feet long or less, you can make a continuous cut along the length. For longer boards, work down a short section two to three feet long at the toe end of the board first, and then move back towards the heel end and work down another section. Continue like this until you reach the heel end of the board. It will take many passes to work the rabbet down to the desired depth, but the work goes fast when the plane iron is sharp.

Cutting a Rabbet Across the Grain

To cut a rabbet across the grain, it is necessary to cut the wood fibres ahead of the plane iron. If not, the plane iron will tear off the fibres, leaving a splintered shoulder.

To cut a cross-grain rabbet with a standard rabbet plane, use a cutting gauge to lay out the joint. A cutting gauge is like a marking gauge, except that it uses a knife blade to cut the line. If you don't have a cutting gauge, use a sharp knife and a straightedge to score the shoulder line. The scored shoulder line will keep the plane iron from tearing out splinters on the face of the board, as long as you don't stray past the line.

When cutting cross-grain, it is a good idea to clamp a piece of scrap to the toe end of the board. This scrap, called a backup board, will help prevent splintering on the edge of the board at the end of the cut.

To cut a cross-grain rabbet with a fillister, use the nicker. The nicker is a small spur that scores a line ahead of the iron. To be effective, the nicker must be kept sharp. You can resharpen it by lightly rubbing it against the edge of a whetstone. Follow its original angle and shape as you sharpen the nicker.

Turn down the nicker by loosening the screw and rotating the nicker until the spur extends below the sole. Set the fence for the desired width and set the depth stop to regulate the depth of the rabbet.

The first step is to score the shoulder line. Do this by placing the plane at the toe end of the board and pulling it rearwards across the face of the board (Illus. 4-11). The nicker will score the shoulder line, but since you are pulling the plane rearwards, the plane iron won't do any cutting. Now, place the plane at the heel end of the board and push it forward to start the cut.

Cross-grain rabbets will be short enough to make in a continuous stroke. Adjust the iron to make a smooth cut. Make repeated passes until the depth stop touches the face of the board (Illus. 4-12).

Illus. 4-12. Making a cross-grain rabbet with a fillister plane. A backup board clamped to the toe end of the work will prevent the plane from splitting the edge of the work.

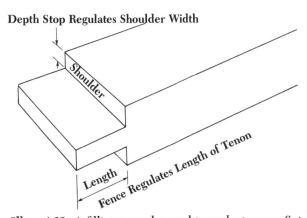

Illus. 4-13. A fillister can be used to make tenons. Set the fence to regulate the length of the tenon. Set the depth stop for the width of the shoulder.

Making Tenons

A fillister can be used to make tenons. The setup is the same as that for making a cross-grain rabbet. Set the fence to regulate the length of the tenon. Set the depth stop for the width of the shoulder (Illus. 4-13). It is faster and more efficient if you cut all of the tenons that are the same size at the same time. Lay all of the boards to be tenoned side by side and add a piece of scrap to the far end to act as a backup board. Clamp all of the boards tightly together. A good way to do this is to lay the boards between a bench stop and the vise.

Scribe the shoulder line with the nicker by pulling the plane rearwards, and then deepen the scribed line with a sharp knife. This will ensure a clean shoulder line. The depth stop may scratch the surface of softwoods. You can protect the face of the board by placing a strip of masking tape on the face on the far side of the scribed line.

Next, plane across all of the boards (Illus. 4-14). Be sure to hold the plane level. If you let the plane tip, the tenon will taper. When you reach the depth stop, unclamp the boards and turn them over. Repeat this procedure to make the other cheek of the tenon.

Making a Stopped Rabbet

A stopped rabbet is used when you don't want the joint to show on the front edge of the project. To make a stopped rabbet, you must use a chisel to cut a small section of the rabbet at the stopped end

Illus. 4-14. When several tenons of the same size are being used on a project, you can make them all at the same time using the fillister plane. Lay all of the boards to be tenoned side by side and add a piece of scrap to the far end to act as a backup board. Clamp all of the boards tightly together.

(Illus. 4-15). This section must be long enough so that the iron will clear the near end before the toe of the plane hits the far end. If you use a bullnose plane, the chiselled section can be quite small. You must chisel a longer section if you use the standard rabbet plane.

Before beginning to chisel, make one pass with the plane. Stop when the cutting edge reaches the desired stopped end. The plane will cut right up to the stopping place on the first pass, but it won't go deeper until you chisel out the end. By making this initial pass with the plane, you have laid out

Illus. 4-15. To make a stopped rabbet, you must use a chisel to cut a small section of the rabbet at the stopped end. If you use a bullnose plane, the cut section can be quite small.

the shoulder for the chiselled-out section. Now, use a chisel to remove the wood at the stopped end of the rabbet.

Once you have cut the short rabbet with the chisel, make the rest of the rabbet with the plane as usual (Illus. 4-16). Start at the edge opposite the stopped end and plane into the cutout section.

Illus. 4-16. Once you have chopped the stopped end of the rabbet with the chisel, make the rest of the rabbet with the plane. Reposition the plane iron to the bullnose position and set the fence and depth stop. Start at the end opposite the stopped end and plane into the chopped-out section.

Using Plow and Dado Planes

Dadoes and grooves can be cut with planes. A groove runs with the grain, and a dado runs across the grain. The plow plane cuts grooves with the grain. A simple wooden plow plane will only cut one size of groove. More complicated versions have interchangeable plane irons, a fence, and a depth stop.

The dado plane cuts dadoes across the grain. It has nickers on both sides of the plane to score the wood ahead of the plane iron. Some dado planes have a skewed iron, because the dado is a cross-grain cut. Since dado joints are usually far away from an edge, no fence is incorporated in most dado planes. Instead, a board is clamped or temporarily tacked to the work to guide the plane.

In the past, a woodworker was likely to have several fixed-size plow and dado planes. This is very convenient when you are using them frequently, because there is no setup time involved when you change from one size to another. Unfortunately, these fixed-size planes are not easily available today, so you will probably end up using one plane with interchangeable plane irons.

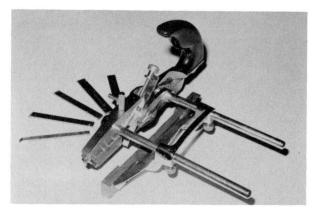

Illus. 4-17. The Record 045C plow plane has a set of interchangeable plane irons, so a number of different sizes of grooves can be made. The plane comes with a nicker on one side; this allows it to function as a fillister as well as a plow. An optional conversion kit is available that adds a nicker to the other side, so the plane can be used to cut dadoes.

The metallic plow/combination plane shown in Illus. 4-17 has a set of interchangeable plane irons, so a number of different sizes of grooves can be made. The plane comes with a nicker on one side; this allows it to function as a fillister as well as a plow. An optional conversion kit is available that adds a nicker to the other side, so the plane can be used to cut dadoes.

Plowing a Groove

A groove can be cut in either the face or edge of the board. The groove for a drawer bottom is made in the face of the board, while the groove for a panel is made in the edge of the frame members. The technique is similar for both operations.

Set up the plow plane by installing the iron that is the required width. You can make odd-sized grooves that fall between the standard sizes of the irons by using a smaller iron and making two overlapping passes, resetting the fence for the second pass. The position of the groove is regulated by the fence. The depth stop controls the depth of the groove.

When cutting the groove on the edge of a board, place the work in a vise; use pegs on the face of the bench to support long boards (Illus. 4-18). You can also use the wedge stop described in Chapter 1 (pages 16–17) to hold a board edge up on the bench top.

When cutting a groove on the face of a board with a plow plane, clamp the board between the end vise and a bench dog, or use a bench stop to hold the work. The plow plane must be able to run out past the end of the board, so position the stop so it will not interfere with the plane. Sideways pressure is used to keep the fence against the edge of the board, so a second bench stop on the far side of the board is advisable.

Unless the board is very long, it is usually best to work the entire groove down in a continuous pass. If this is inconvenient because of the length of the board, you can work it down in sections. Start at the toe end of the board and work down a short section. Then step rearwards and work down the next section, letting the plane run out into the section previously plowed. Make multiple passes until the depth stop touches the work.

Illus. 4-18. When plowing a groove on the edge of a board, place the work in a vise; use pegs on the face of the bench to support long boards.

Cutting Barefaced Tongue-and-Groove Joints

If you have studied the joints in antique furniture, you may have noticed that the barefaced tongue-and-groove joint is used extensively in situations where modern woodworkers would probably have used a simple dado (Illus. 4-19). There is a practical reason for this. A wooden dado plane only cuts one size of dado. Wood that has been surfaced by hand can be various thicknesses. In order to achieve a tight-fitting joint with a minimum number of dado planes, the barefaced tongue-and-groove joint was used. The dado was cut first, and then a rabbet plane was used to make the tongue on the mating board. Since the depth of the rabbet can be easily changed, the tongue can be made to fit into the dado snugly, no matter what the thickness of the board.

To make a dado using the Record 045C plane, install a plane iron of the desired width and set its nicker to score the wood slightly deeper than the plane iron depth (Illus. 4-20).

For most applications, it is advisable to use a barefaced tongue-and-groove joint. Note that the joint shown and illustrated in this section has a tongue that really fits into a dado, but it is still called a tongue-and-groove joint. This joint makes it possible to account for variations in the thickness of the wood.

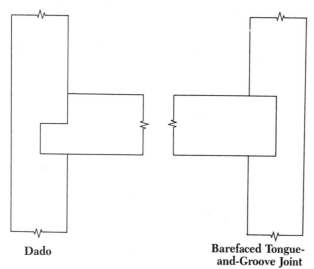

Illus. 4-21. Dadoes are usually too far away from the end of the board for the fence to be used. To guide the plane, clamp a guide board to the work at the location of the dado. The guide board must be thin enough so that it won't interfere with the plane; ⅛-inch hardboard works well. Make the guide board wide enough so that the clamps can be placed where they won't interfere with the plane. If a few nail holes in the face of the board aren't objectionable, you can use a narrow strip of wood and tack it in place with small nails instead of using clamps.

Illus. 4-19. The barefaced tongue-and-groove joint is used extensively in antique furniture. It is still the best choice when using planes to make the joints. A simple dado joint must be cut to the exact width to fit the mating board. If the board thickness doesn't match the standard-size dado blade, then you must use a smaller blade and make two passes. When the barefaced tongue-and-groove joint is used, a standard-size dado is cut first, and then a rabbet plane is used to make the tongue on the mating board. Since the depth of the rabbet can be easily changed, the tongue can be made to fit into the dado snugly, no matter what thickness the board is.

To make a barefaced tongue-and-groove joint, make a dado that is smaller than the thickness of the board. Then clamp a guide board to the work at the location of the dado. The guide board must be thin enough so that it won't interfere with the plane; ⅛-inch hardboard works well (Illus. 4-21). The depth stop will contact the guide board instead of the face of the board, so set it ⅛ inch higher than the desired depth of cut. Usually, the dado should be cut one-half the thickness of the board. It is a good idea to place a scrap board next to the far edge of the work. This board will help to prevent splintering as the plane exits the cut.

Score the shoulder lines with the nicker first by placing the plane against the guide board and pulling it rearwards across the face of the board (Illus. 4-22). This will allow the nicker to score the shoulders, but the plane iron won't cut into the wood because it is going rearwards. Now, push the plane forward and make the first cut. Make multiple passes over the work until the dado is the desired depth (Illus. 4-23).

Illus. 4-20. To make a dado using the Record 045C plane, remove the original blade clamp, replace it with the optional sliding section, and install the desired plane iron. Set the nicker by loosening the clamp screw, lowering the nicker, then retightening the screw. The nicker should score the wood slightly deeper than the plane iron depth.

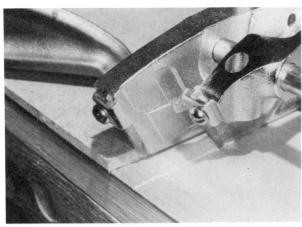

Illus. 4-22. Score the shoulders of the dado with the nicker. Place the plane against the guide board and pull it rearwards across the face of the board.

Illus. 4-23. Once the shoulders have been scored, push the plane forward to make the cut. Make multiple passes over the work until the dado is the desired depth.

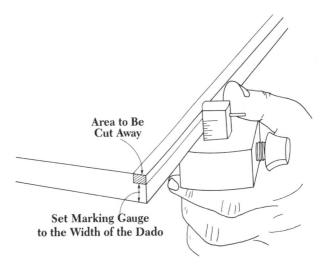

Illus. 4-24. The depth of the rabbet depends on the thickness of the board. Gauge a line on the end of the board with the marking gauge set to the width of the dado, and the fence against the face of the board opposite the face to be rabbeted.

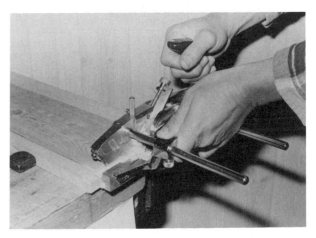

Illus. 4-25. You can use a rabbet plane, a fillister, or the plow combination plane set up as a fillister to cut a rabbet on the end of the mating board of the barefaced tongue-and-groove joint.

Next, make the barefaced tongue on the mating board. You can use a rabbet plane, a fillister, or the plow/combination plane set up as a fillister to cut a rabbet on the end of the board. The rabbet should be as wide as the depth of the dado. The depth of the rabbet depends on the thickness of the board. Gauge a line on the end of the board with the marking gauge set to the width of the dado, and the fence against the face of the board opposite the face to be rabbeted (Illus. 4-24). Now, work down the rabbet to the gauged line (Illus. 4-25). Test-fit the tongue in the dado. It should fit snugly.

Cutting Stopped Dadoes and Grooves

A stopped joint can be used to hide the joint. To make a stopped dado or groove, it is necessary to cut a short section of the dado or groove with a chisel. This section should start where the dado or groove will stop, and it should be long enough to allow the plane iron to pass into the cutout section

before the toe of the plane hits the end of the dado or groove.

An easy way to align the chiselled section with the groove is to make one pass with the plane before chopping with the chisel. Stop planing when the cutting edge reaches the mark for the stopped end. Use this shallow groove as a guide when you chop with the chisel (Illus. 4-26). After you have chopped out a section at the end, plane the rest of the groove as usual, starting at the end opposite the stopped cut (Illus. 4-27).

Illus. 4-26. To make a stopped dado or groove, it is necessary to cut a short section of the dado or groove with a chisel. This section should start where the dado or groove will stop, and it should be long enough to allow the plane iron to pass into the cut-out section before the toe of the plane hits the end of the dado or groove.

Illus. 4-27. After you have chopped out a section at the end, plow the groove as usual, starting at the end opposite the stopped cut.

Chapter 5
SPECIALTY PLANES

Planes have been adapted for a variety of specialized uses. In earlier days, many different crafts had special planes for specific jobs. Some, like the cooper's topping plane that is curved to fit the top of a barrel, are so specialized they are of little use to general woodworkers. However, some of the specialty planes have many uses. For example, the wheelwright's spokeshave is very versatile and can be used whenever odd-shaped parts need to be smoothed.

In this chapter, I have grouped together several specialty planes that are of use to general woodworkers. At the time of this writing, the plane types listed in this chapter were still in production, but some may require special ordering through catalogues. You can also find specialty planes at used tool shops, flea markets, and garage sales, but you will have to search for them. Interest in used tools is increasing, and a number of shops specialize in them.

Compass Planes

The compass plane is used to plane convex or concave shapes. Wooden compass planes were made in the past. The wooden planes can only be used on the one curvature they were made for. The metallic compass plane can be adjusted for many different curves, both convex and concave (Illus. 5-1).

The metallic compass plane uses the same type of adjustment mechanism as a standard bench plane, so the iron adjustments are made in the same way as you would normally make them on a bench plane. The knob on top of the plane is used to adjust the curvature of the flexible steel sole. To set the sole, place the plane on the surface to be planed and adjust the knob until the sole rests on the surface uniformly.

For best results, you should plane with the grain. On curved surfaces, the grain direction will change as you pass the crest of the curve (Illus. 5-2). You should change the direction of the plane to compensate for this, so that you are always planing with the grain. Hold the plane parallel with the edges of the board. You cannot skew the plane as you would with a normal bench plane.

Gutter Planes

The gutter plane was originally developed for making the trough in a wooden gutter. It has a convex sole and iron (Illus. 5-3). In woodworker's terminology, any long trough-shaped area is called a gutter. The gutter plane is useful whenever a gutter is needed. The gutter plane can be used to make large architectural mouldings such as cove moulding (Illus. 5-4).

The gutter plane is very similar in appearance to a wooden jack plane. It is adjusted with a mallet, using the procedure given in Chapter 1. Hitting the heel raises the iron, and hitting the toe or tapping down on the iron lowers it.

To use a gutter plane, clamp the work to the bench and place the plane at the heel end of the board. Take a light cut along the length of the board. You must guide the plane carefully for this first cut. Once there is a small gutter, the plane

Illus. 5-1. The compass plane is used to plane convex or concave shapes. (Photo courtesy of Record Tools.)

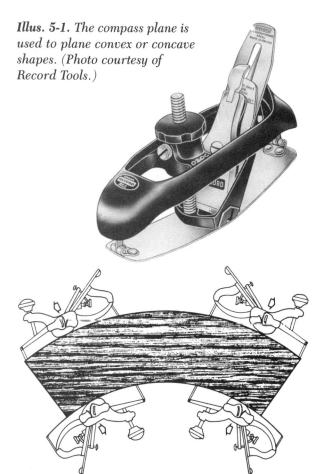

Illus. 5-2. On curved surfaces, the grain direction will change as you pass the crest of the curve. You should change the direction of the plane to compensate for this, so that you are always planing with the grain. In this illustration, you can see that you should plane towards the middle of an inside curve and away from the middle of an outside curve.

Illus. 5-3. The gutter plane was originally developed for making the trough in a wooden gutter. It has a convex sole and iron.

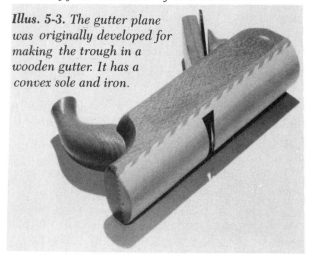

Illus. 5-4. The gutter plane can be used to make large architectural mouldings such as this cove moulding. This type of moulding is often used as a crown moulding. More complex crown mouldings can be made by using other planes in conjunction with the gutter plane.

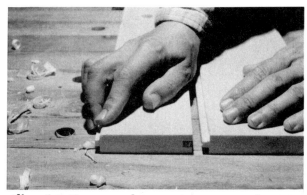

Illus. 5-5. To use a gutter plane, clamp the work to the bench and place the plane at the heel end of the board. Make a light cut along the length of the board. You must guide the plane carefully for this first cut. Once there is a small gutter, the plane will follow the previous cuts, making it easier to guide. In this illustration, I am making the cove moulding shown in Illus. 5-4. After making the gutter, the next step is to bevel the sides so the moulding can be attached at a 45-degree angle to the wall.

Illus. 5-6. Tongue-and-groove joints are used to join boards together without glue to allow for dimensional changes caused by changes in moisture content of the wood. Match planes can be used to make the tongue-and-groove joint.

will follow the previous cuts, making it easier to guide (Illus. 5-5). If you have trouble getting the cut straight, clamp a board to the work to guide the plane for the first few passes. Position the board so that it rubs against the cheek of the plane stock.

Match Planes

Match planes are used to make tongue-and-groove joints (Illus. 5-6). Two planes are used, one to cut the tongue and the other to cut the groove. These two planes are a matched set; that is why these planes are called match planes.

Wooden match planes are still being produced, but you may need to order them through a special mail-order catalogue (Illus. 5-7). You may find some used wooden match planes at a flea market or used-tool shop.

When you buy used planes, make sure that they are really a matched set. If they are not matched, the tongue may not fit into the groove or the boards may not be flush when assembled. The universal combination planes described in Chap-

ter 6 can also do the work of match planes.

Wooden match planes are adjusted in much the same way as described in Chapter 1 for traditional planes. To adjust the iron, strike the heel of the plane to raise the iron and tap the top of the iron to lower it. Always tap down the wedge after making an adjustment.

To sharpen the iron, remove the wedge by striking the heel hard with a mallet. If this doesn't loosen the wedge, cushion the wedge between two blocks of scrap wood and clamp the end of the wedge in a vise. Now, use a mallet to drive the plane away from the wedge. This method is preferable to hitting the lower side of the notch on the wedge, because it prevents damage to the wedge.

These planes usually have a built-in fence. The fence is not adjustable, so separate sets of match planes are needed for various board thicknesses.

It is common practice to cut a groove on one edge of the board and a tongue on the other, but I have seen examples of antiques where the boards alternate; that is, one board has tongues on both edges, and the other has grooves on both edges. The first and last boards will only need to be worked on one edge; one will have a tongue on one edge, and the other a groove on one edge.

Illus. **5-7** (**left**). *Match planes are used to make tongue-and-groove joints. Two planes are used, one to cut the tongue and the other to cut the groove. These planes have a built-in fence. The fence is not adjustable, so separate sets of match planes are needed for various board thicknesses.*

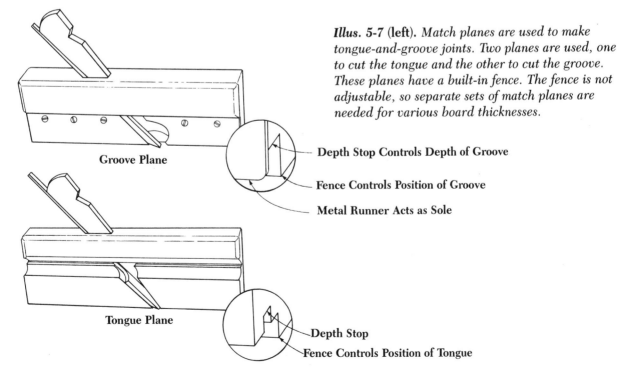

Groove Plane

Depth Stop Controls Depth of Groove

Fence Controls Position of Groove

Metal Runner Acts as Sole

Tongue Plane

Depth Stop

Fence Controls Position of Tongue

2. Lift the heel on the backstroke.

4. After the tongue has been formed along the entire length, make a pass along the full length of the board with the plane.

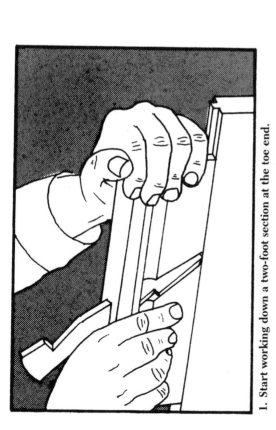

1. Start working down a two-foot section at the toe end.

3. After the first section is done, move back a step and work down another two-foot section.

Illus. 5-8. When making a tongue-and-groove joint on long boards, you can use this procedure to make the cut instead of walking the full length of the board on each pass.

The procedure for using both planes is similar (Illus. 5-8). Support long boards with pegs on the front of the bench. Start about two feet behind the toe end of the board. Hold the plane's fence against the face of the board to guide the cut. Work down a section about two feet long. The work will go faster if you don't take a cut that is too rank. A fine cut requires less effort and produces a better tongue.

You will need to make about 20 strokes to work down to the depth stop. Once you get into a rhythm, the work goes rapidly. On the back stroke, raise the heel of the plane so that the iron is not in contact with the wood. You can leave the toe and fence against the work as you slide the plane back, so that you won't need to reposition the plane for each stroke.

Once you have worked down the first section, move back a step towards the heel end of the board and work down another section. When you have worked down the entire length of the board, take a full-length pass by walking with the plane along the entire length of the board. This will even out any irregularities in the cut.

Illus. 5-9. The simplest type of moulding planes are called hollows and rounds. The hollow plane shown in this photograph has a concave profile. The round plane has a convex profile. They are used together to make more complex mouldings or individually to make simple mouldings such as quarter rounds and coves.

Moulding Planes

Up until the late 1800's, a woodworker usually had a chest that was filled with different moulding planes. Moulding planes are used to make mouldings, which are decorative recessed or relieved surfaces. The simplest types of moulding planes are called *hollows* and *rounds*. The hollow plane has a concave profile (Illus. 5-9). The round plane has a convex profile. They are used together to make up more complex mouldings or individually to make simple mouldings such as quarter rounds and coves. As far as I know, rounds are the only moulding planes that are still in production. Hollows and rounds are still commonly available on the used tool market at reasonable prices.

More complex moulding planes can produce intricate mouldings in a single step. You can still find some of these at a flea market, but since they are now collector's items, they are getting more expensive. A used tool shop will have a better

Illus. 5-10. By using hollows and rounds in conjunction with a rabbet or a plow plane, you can make virtually any moulding profile. In this photograph, a hollow plane is being used to finish up a cornice moulding. The type of curve used in this moulding is called a cyma recta. It consists of a convex section that makes a smooth transition to a concave section. The cyma recta can be made by using a round plane to cut the concave section and a hollow to cut the convex section. The flat fillets can be cut with a rabbet plane. (A fillet is a flat section on a moulding used to separate a section of the moulding.)

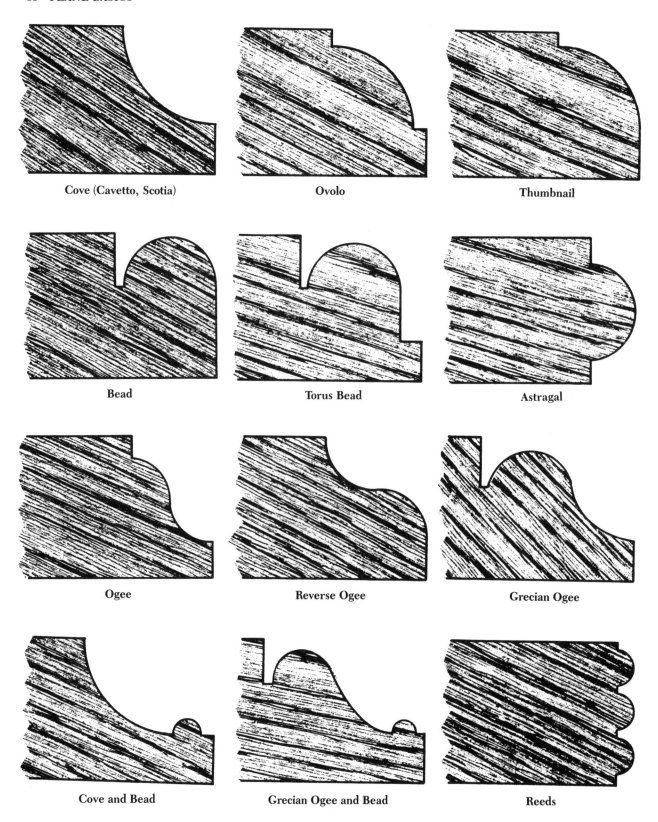

Cove (Cavetto, Scotia) Ovolo Thumbnail

Bead Torus Bead Astragal

Ogee Reverse Ogee Grecian Ogee

Cove and Bead Grecian Ogee and Bead Reeds

Illus. 5-11. These are a few of the many mouldings that can be cut with hand planes.

selection. Avoid buying damaged planes or high-priced collectible planes.

Hollows and rounds are very versatile tools. At first glance, it may seem that they would only be useful for a few jobs, but as you use them more, you will find many uses for them. The most obvious uses for a hollow plane are rounding over corners and making quarter-round moulding. The round plane can be used to make cove moulding.

If you look carefully at most mouldings, you will notice that they consist of coves and rounded sections put together in various combinations. By using hollows and rounds in conjunction with a rabbet or a plow plane, you can make virtually any moulding profile (Illus. 5-10).

Most hollows and rounds are not a complete quarter of a circle. They are closer to one-sixth of a circle. This makes them more versatile, because you can make a small or large arc. To make an arc larger than the arc of the plane, a quarter round for example, change the position of the plane for each stroke so that the entire area is planed.

Common hollows and rounds don't have a fence or any other type of guide. To guide the plane, wrap your fingers around the stock so that they rest against the edge of the board, and let your fingers act as a fence. Start the cut about one foot from the toe end of the board and plane a few strokes. Then move back a little on each subsequent stroke. The plane will follow the original path made by the first few strokes, and you can gradually work your way to a full-length stroke along the entire surface of the board.

One of the biggest advantages of common hollows and rounds is that they can be used in either direction. This means that if there is a change in the direction of the wood grain, you can reverse the direction of the plane to prevent tear-out. More complex moulding planes can't be reversed like this, so they may leave some tear-out. If you have a hollow or round that is the right size, you can smooth up rough areas left by other moulding planes by going over the area with the hollow or round, planing in the opposite direction.

A more complex moulding plane has a cutter that is shaped to the reverse profile of the desired moulding. Illus. 5-11 shows a few of the more popular moulding profiles. The sole of the plane is also shaped to the profile of the cutter. Moulding planes other than hollows and rounds also have two flat areas on the sole; one is the fence, and the other the stop (Illus. 5-12).

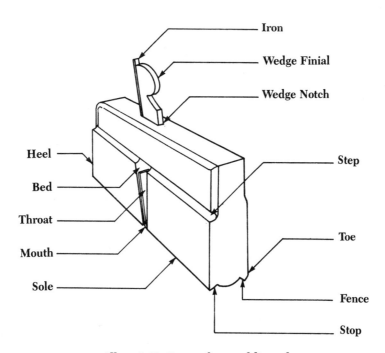

Illus. 5-12. Parts of a moulding plane.

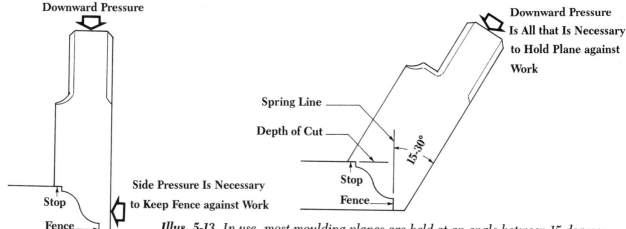

Illus. 5-13. In use, most moulding planes are held at an angle between 15 degrees and 30 degrees. This type of plane is called a sprung plane. The sprung plane shown on the right is easier to use than one that is not sprung, shown on the left. Downward pressure on a sprung plane holds the fence against the work and provides the downward pressure necessary for cutting. When using a plane that is not sprung, you must apply side pressure to hold the fence against the work while applying downward pressure to make the cut.

In use, most moulding planes are held at an angle between 15 degrees and 30 degrees. A plane that can be held at this angle is called a *sprung plane* (Illus. 5-13). A sprung plane is easier to use than one that is not sprung. Downward pressure on a sprung plane holds the fence against the work and gives the downward pressure necessary for cutting. When using a plane that is not sprung, you must apply side pressure to hold the fence against the work while applying downward pressure to make the cut.

There may be one or two lines scribed into the fore end of a sprung plane. These are called *spring lines*. They help you position the plane. Hold the plane so that the spring lines are parallel to the edge and face of the board.

Wooden moulding planes are adjusted with a mallet. Strike the heel of the plane to raise the iron, and tap the top of the iron to lower it. After making an adjustment, tighten the wedge by tapping it with a mallet. It is usually best to set the iron fine. A rank iron will be difficult to use, and tear-out or chatter marks will mar the surface of the moulding.

To remove the iron for sharpening, remove the wedge using the procedure described for match planes. You will need a special type of whetstone called a slipstone to do the sharpening. Slipstones

come in several shapes; one of the most useful has a teardrop-shaped cross section. This type of slipstone has a large round edge, a small round edge, and two flat surfaces. Slipstones can be made from natural or man-made materials.

Ceramic stones are also available. These stones are made into long, thin "files." You can get a set of these ceramic files that includes files with round, triangular, square, and teardrop shapes. You will have to sharpen each small section of the cutting edge separately. Select the edge of the slipstone that most closely conforms to the profile of the cutter, and hold the stone at the same angle as the existing bevel (Illus. 5-14). After honing all of the bevelled edge, back off the wire edge on a flat whetstone. I recommend that a novice only buy a used moulding plane if the iron is in good condition and only in need of minor honing. If it needs extensive regrinding, the procedure is too difficult for the novice.

The process of cutting a moulding is called *sticking* or *striking*. The board that the moulding is cut into is called a *stick*. When you are finished, the moulding has been stuck or struck. Choose the wood carefully. Clear, straight-grained stock will give you the best results.

To begin sticking, place the board face-up on the bench and clamp it. Hold the plane so that the

Illus. 5-14. To sharpen a moulding plane iron, you will need a special type of whetstone called a slipstone. Slipstones come in several shapes; one of the most useful is the teardrop shape shown here.

fence rests against the corner of the board. Adjust the tilt of the plane until the fence rests flat against the edge of the board. The plane is now sprung correctly.

For short boards, simply place the toe of the plane on the heel end of the board and plane all the way to the toe end in a single pass. It may take 30 or more passes to work the plane down to the stop. The shavings will get progressively wider as you work down. When the stop hits the face of the board, the moulding is completely stuck.

When the board is too long to stick in a single stroke, you can walk along with the plane. Another method is to start at the toe end of the board. Work down a section that is two or three feet long. Stop planing slightly before the stop will touch the face. Now, move slightly back towards the heel end of the board and work down the next two-to-three-foot section. Working rearwards like this is necessary so that the toe of the plane won't hit an unstuck section of wood. Continue working down small sections until you reach the heel end of the board. Make the final few strokes the full length of the stick. Walk along as you push the plane.

When the design of the moulding requires the removal of much wood to get down to the moulding profile, you can remove most of the waste with a jack plane. Hold the plane on the approximate angle of the base line of the moulding and plane down until most of the waste has been removed. Be careful not to plane too far; if you do, some of the details of the moulding can't be fully worked.

Radius Planes

The radius plane is a plane used to round or chamfer (cut a bevel on) the edges of a board (Illus. 5-15). The radius plane is a handy tool when the style of the project requires rounded or chamfered edges. It gives more uniform results than you can get with sandpaper.

The radius plane is a modern adaptation of the traditional wooden moulding plane. It has two cutters; the first one makes a rough cut, and the second one makes a finer cut, leaving a smooth surface in a single pass. Like a traditional moulding plane, the radius plane is sprung, but it is held at a 45-degree angle, which is steeper than the 15-to-30-degree angles that traditional planes use. the plane can be adjusted from a 1/16-inch cutting width to a 1/4-inch cutting width. There are two types of radius planes available: One has a curved cutter for rounding over an edge, and the other has a straight cutter for making a chamfer.

Illus. 5-15. The radius plane is a plane used to round or chamfer the edges of a board.

An allen wrench is used to make adjustments. There are setscrews on both sides of each cutter. These setscrews lock the adjustment and center the cutter. A third screw on top of the plane adjusts the height of the cutter (Illus. 5-16).

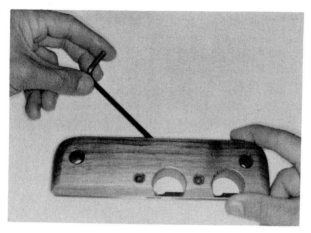

Illus. 5-16. *An allen wrench is used to adjust the radius plane. There are setscrews on both sides of each cutter (iron). These setscrews lock the adjustment and center the cutter. A third screw on top of the plane adjusts the height of the cutter.*

Begin adjusting the radius plane by loosening the side setscrews. Then adjust the cutter up or down, using the screw on top. The rear cutter should be set slightly lower than the front one. You can tell if the adjustment is correct by making a test cut. The shavings from the front cutter should be about twice as thick as the shavings from the rear cutter.

You can control the amount of wood removed on each pass by the angle at which you hold the plane. You will get a smoother cut if you make several light cuts. Hold the plane at about a 30-degree angle for the first pass. This will lift the cutters away from the edge enough to make a light cut. On each subsequent pass, increase the angle until the plane is at 45 degrees and both sides of the brass sole are resting on the wood.

Like all planes, the radius plane will produce a smoother cut if you plane into uphill grain. Pay attention to the first pass. If the wood tears, plane in the other direction for the rest of the strokes.

Rounders

A rounder is used to make dowels or round stock. It works on the same principle as a pencil sharpener (Illus. 5-17). This is a traditional tool that has been around since the 1700's. Rounders can be used to make broom handles, rake handles, and even simple chairs and stools, without a lathe. Even if you have a lathe, a rounder can be useful when you need to make something that is longer than your lathe can handle. You can still buy new rounders. You may also be able to find used ones on the used tool market.

Illus. 5-17. *A rounder, shown on the right and on the bottom, is used to make dowels or round stock. A pointer, shown on the left, tapers the end of a dowel. These planes work like a pencil sharpener.*

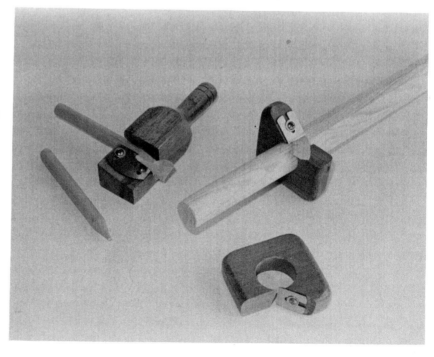

To use the rounder, you must cut the wood to the approximate size and then chamfer the corners with a bench plane or a drawknife. When you can fit the large end of the rounder over the end of the wood, you are ready to use the rounder. For small dowels, you can hold the rounder in one hand and the wood in the other. Twist the wood or the rounder, whichever is most comfortable for you. For larger-diameter dowels, it may be necessary to place either the rounder or one end of the wood in the vise and use both hands to twist the rounder or the wood. The rounder is cutting cross-grain, so the surface will usually be a little rough. You can smooth it with a spokeshave.

The *baller* and the *pointer* are two other tools that work on the same principle and are often used in conjunction with a rounder. The baller rounds over the end of a dowel. It can be used to make a rounded end on a rake handle or something similar. The pointer tapers the end of a dowel. It can be used to make a sharp point like that needed on a tent stake, or to reduce the diameter of the end of a larger dowel so that it can be fitted into a smaller hole. This can be useful in chairmaking.

Router Planes

The router plane is used to smooth the bottom of a recess (cut indentation in a piece of wood). It can be used to smooth the bottom of a dado that has been cut with a saw and chisel. The router plane can smooth gains for hinges or locks. (A gain is the shallow recess cut into a board so that the leaf of a hinge or the case of a cabinet lock will be flush with the surface.) It can also be used to smooth the bottom of a recess for an inlay or to smooth the background of a carved area. The wooden version of a router plane is called an old woman's tooth. Both metallic and wooden router planes are still available. Unlike most planes, the router plane is usually pulled towards you rather than pushed away.

The router plane consists of a wide base and a cutter that can be adjusted to project below the base. The cutter of the tool is called the *bit*. Bits come in several sizes and are interchangeable.

Some bits are made for rough cutting, and others for smoothing.

The bit can be installed in the normal position used for routers, in the middle of the base for most work. When it is necessary to make a stopped cut, place the bit in the bullnose position at the rear of the base. Some router planes also have provisions for a fence.

The plane shown in Illus. 5-18 has an open mouth. The open mouth gives you better visibility when working on the face of a board. When making a groove on the edge of a board, you need to use a closed-mouth plane, because the sides of the base won't be in contact with the wood to support the plane. You can convert an open-mouthed plane to a closed-mouth plane by installing the removable shoe in the mouth.

While it is possible to make the entire cut with a router plane by adjusting the bit progressively lower on each stroke, it is usually more practical to remove most of the wood with a chisel, and then use the router plane to do the final smoothing. Using a dado as an example, the following procedure is used. First, use a backsaw to make the cheek cut of the dado (Illus. 5-19). Next, use a chisel, bevel-side down, to remove most of the waste (Illus. 5-20). Now, set the bit of the router plane to the desired depth and place it in the dado. Pull the plane across the board (Illus. 5-21). It will take several passes to clean up a wide dado. For a smoother cutting action, you can skew the plane up to 30 degrees.

You can add a wooden extension base when smoothing a large recessed area. This can be very useful when smoothing the background of a large carving. Make the extension base out of ¼- or ½-inch plywood. Drill a hole in the middle, for the bit. There are two holes in the router base in which screws can be placed to attach the extension base.

When making grooves, you can use the fence to guide the router plane. The router plane is not as efficient for making grooves as the plow plane, but it has one distinct advantage: The fence has a curved side that makes it possible to follow a curved edge.

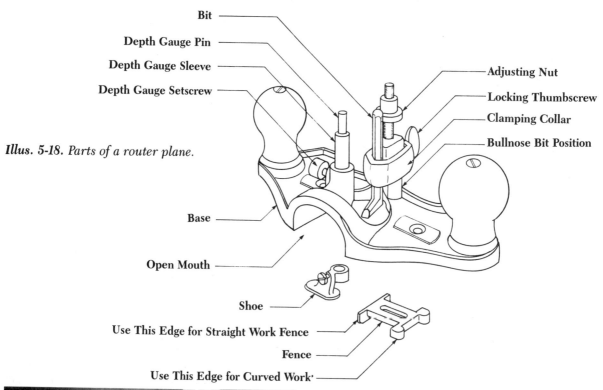

Bit

Depth Gauge Pin

Depth Gauge Sleeve

Depth Gauge Setscrew

Adjusting Nut

Locking Thumbscrew

Clamping Collar

Bullnose Bit Position

Illus. 5-18. Parts of a router plane.

Base

Open Mouth

Shoe

Use This Edge for Straight Work Fence

Fence

Use This Edge for Curved Work

Illus. 5-19 (left). The router plane can be used to smooth a dado that is cut with a saw and chisel. First, use a backsaw to make the cheek cut of the dado, as shown here.

Illus. 5-20 (below left). Use a chisel, bevel-side down, to remove most of the waste between the shoulder cuts.

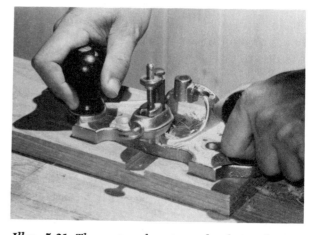

Illus. 5-21. The router plane is used to bring the dado to finished depth and smooth the bottom of the cut.

If you are using an open-mouthed plane to cut a groove, you must install the shoe to support the front of the plane before you can cut a groove on the edge of a board. To install the shoe, raise the bit above the base, place the shoe in the mouth, and set the plane base down on a flat surface. Adjust the shoe so that it is resting on the flat surface along with the base of the plane; then tighten the shoe setscrew. Next, install the bit of the correct width. The standard-size bits are either ¼ or ½ inch. If you need a different-size groove, you can use a bit that is smaller than the desired finished size and make two side-by-side cuts.

To set the bit depth for the first cut, loosen the thumbscrew on the clamping collar and turn the adjusting nut until the bit is flush with the base. Then turn the nut one additional turn and tighten the thumbscrew. Now, install the fence and set it to the correct distance.

Place the plane on the edge of the work, with the plane's fence against the face and its shoe resting on the edge. The bit should be off the end of the board. Now, pull the plane into the work and make a pass along the entire length of the board. Before starting the next stroke, loosen the thumbscrew and turn the adjusting nut one full turn to lower the bit. Retighten the thumbscrew and make another pass over the board. Continue in this manner until you reach the desired depth.

Some planes have a built-in depth gauge (Illus. 5-22). This is a sliding pin that will fall into the groove as it is cut. A setscrew holds the outer sleeve of the depth gauge in position. To set the depth gauge, loosen the setscrew and move the sleeve up or down until the bottom of the pin projects the desired amount below the base. Now, tighten the setscrew. When you place the plane on the work, the pin will be forced up and its top will protrude above the sleeve. As you plane, the pin will fall down into the groove. When the top of the pin is flush with the top of the sleeve, you have reached the desired depth.

To make a curved groove, turn the fence around so that the curved side is against the work (Illus. 5-23). This side will work with both concave and convex surfaces. This setup can be used to make a groove in the edge of a bent board or in the face of a board that has a curved edge.

If the board has been steam-bent, then the grain will run in the same direction all along the cut. (Steam-bent wood starts out as a straight board. It is softened by heat and moisture from steam, and then bent to a curve. Since it originally was a straight board, the grain direction will follow the curve.) When the board has been sawed to a curve, then the grain will change directions as you pass the crest of the curve. In extreme cases, it may be necessary to stop cutting at this point and reposition the plane on the other end of the

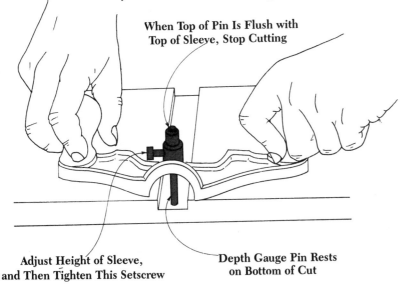

When Top of Pin Is Flush with Top of Sleeve, Stop Cutting

Adjust Height of Sleeve, and Then Tighten This Setscrew

Depth Gauge Pin Rests on Bottom of Cut

Illus. 5-22. The depth gauge on the router plane works differently from the depth gauges on the other planes. The pin is free to slide up and down. As you make the cut, the pin slides down to rest on the bottom of the cut. The sleeve can be adjusted up or down to act as a reference point. You can tell how much more you have to cut by how far the pin extends above the sleeve. When the pin is flush with the top of the sleeve, the cut has reached its correct depth.

Illus. **5-23.** *The router plane can be used to cut grooves along a curved edge. The fence is reversible; one side is straight, and the other side is shaped to follow a curved edge. This side of the fence will follow either convex or concave edges. When making the groove close to the edge, it is also necessary to install the shoe in the mouth of the plane to support the front of the base.*

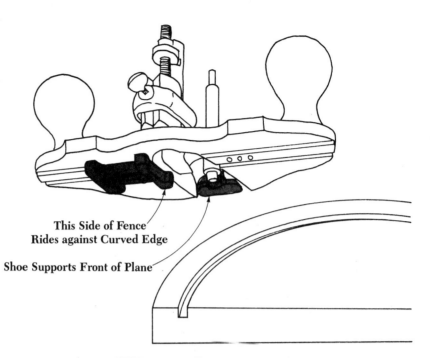

This Side of Fence
Rides against Curved Edge

Shoe Supports Front of Plane

board and cut from the opposite direction. This will necessitate repositioning the fence on the opposite side of the plane.

Stopped grooves can be made with the router plane. To make a stopped groove, first chop a short section of the groove at the stopped end with a mortise chisel. Now, start at the opposite end and make the groove as usual, stopping when the bit reaches the mortised area. You can make a groove that is stopped at both ends, if you chop a mortise at each end of the groove. Begin the cut with the bit inside one of the mortises and stop when you reach the other.

After reading the directions above, you can probably see that although the router plane can be used to make dadoes and grooves, a plow plane is really better suited for the job. The best use for a router plane is for levelling the bottom of a large recess. This is a task that no other plane can do. It is particularly useful for inlay work. (An inlay is a decorative piece set into a surface.) In this case, the depth of the cut is small, usually 1⁄16 inch or less. Therefore, you can make the cut in two passes, the first to remove most of the wood, and the second to smooth the surface. This avoids the repeated depth adjustments at the beginning of each pass needed to make a deep groove.

Use a sharp knife to cut the outline of the inlay

Illus. **5-24.** *The best use for a router plane is for levelling the bottom of a large recess. This is a task that no other plane can do. It is particularly useful for inlay work.*

on the face of the board. Then place the router plane on the work. Remove the waste by making several parallel passes with the grain. Then set the bit for the final depth and take a fine cut for the final pass (Illus. 5-24).

Spokeshaves

The spokeshave was originally a wheelwright's tool used to smooth wooden wheel spokes. Even

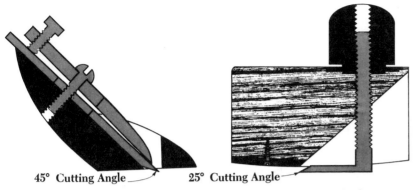

45° Cutting Angle

Metallic Spokeshave

25° Cutting Angle

Wooden Spokeshave

Illus. 5-25. The metallic spoke-shave is very different from the wooden spokeshave. This cross section shows that the iron of a metallic spokeshave is bedded just like the iron on a plane. The wooden spokeshave has the low-angle cutting action of a draw-knife.

though the need for wooden wheels is considerably less than it was a century ago, the spokeshave is still a popular tool. It is very versatile, and can be used on a variety of projects that are not even remotely related to wooden wheels. A spokeshave is particularly useful in chairmaking. It is very useful for smoothing the sculpted shapes of modern furniture.

Metallic and wooden spokeshaves are both available. The metallic spokeshave is very different from the wooden spokeshave (Illus. 5-25). The metallic spokeshave is truly a plane. Its iron is bedded at the same angle as the iron of a bench plane, and its cutting edge protrudes from a mouth in the sole.

Metallic spokeshaves are available with either a straight blade or a half-round blade. Straight-blade spokeshaves are most versatile. Half-round spokeshaves can only be used on curves with a small diameter (such as a wagon wheel spoke). Metallic spokeshaves are easily available. If you can't buy them locally, most mail-order woodworking supply companies sell several types.

The spokeshave should be set for a very fine cut. Some spokeshaves have a nut-and-screw adjustment mechanism that makes accurate adjustment easy (Illus. 5-26). Others only have a thumbscrew to hold the blade. With this type, you must loosen the thumbscrew and slide the blade up or down with your fingers to make adjustments.

The wooden spokeshave, on the other hand, is more like a drawknife than a plane. Its blade is set at a low angle. Its wooden stock helps to position the blade so the cutting action is more uniform

Illus. 5-26. This metallic spokeshave has a nut-and-screw adjustment mechanism that makes accurate adjustment easy. (Photo courtesy of Record Tools.)

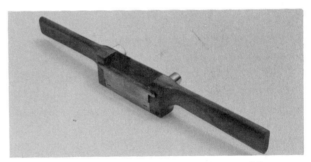

Illus. 5-27. The wooden spokeshave is more like a drawknife than a plane. The blade is set at a low angle. Many experienced woodworkers prefer the wooden spokeshave.

than that of a drawknife, but it retains the slicing action of a drawknife as opposed to the planing action of the metallic spokeshave. Many experienced woodworkers prefer the wooden spoke-shave (Illus. 5-27).

You would normally push a spokeshave away from your body, but you can also turn it around and pull it towards you if that is more convenient for the job at hand. Plane with the grain, to get the smoothest cut. On curved surfaces, the grain direction can change abruptly. Study the grain to determine the best way to work.

Chapter 6
UNIVERSAL COMBINATION PLANES

Towards the end of the 1800's, inventors were developing multi-purpose planes that could do the jobs of several traditional planes. The final step in this evolution was the "universal combination plane" that can do the job of many specialty planes. These planes are known by several names: combination planes, multi-planes, and universal planes.

Technically, any plane that can be used with cutters of different sizes is a universal plane. For example, a plow plane with interchangeable cutters of different sizes can be called a universal plow plane. A plane that can be used for more than one job is called a combination plane. The planes described in this chapter are correctly called universal combination planes, because they can be used with a wide range of cutter sizes and they perform the functions of several specialty planes.

In this chapter, I will discuss three universal combination planes (Illus. 6-1). The simplest is the Record 045C plow/combination plane. With the addition of the K050C conversion kit, this plane becomes a true universal combination plane. The second actually includes two very similar planes: the Stanley #45 and the Record Multi-Plane. The most complex universal combination plane is the Stanley #55. This plane is similar to the #45, but it includes sole runners that can be adjusted vertically. This improvement makes the #55 able to produce a wider range of mouldings than the other planes.

The Record 045C is still being produced. The Stanley #45 and the Record Multi-Plane are no longer being produced by the original manufacturers, but reproductions are available. A group of former Record employees formed the Clifton Company to manufacture some of the planes that have been discontinued by Record; they make a reproduction of the Multi-Plane. The Stanley #55 is out of production. I don't know of any reproductions of the Stanley #55 currently available. I have included information on the #55 because there are still many of these planes available on the used tool market. Hopefully, someone will soon make a reasonably priced reproduction.

Universal combination planes are a monument to nineteenth-century ingenuity. They can make rabbets, dadoes, grooves, tongue-and-groove joints, and many types of mouldings. They are all similar in some respects. Instead of a solid sole, the plane rides on runners that look a little like ice-skate blades. Because of this resemblance, they are often called "skates." The runners can be adjusted to the width of the cut being made. Interchangeable cutters are used. The cutters come in a variety of sizes and profiles. Various fences and stops make the plane adaptable to many different applications.

The Record 045C, the Stanley #45, and the

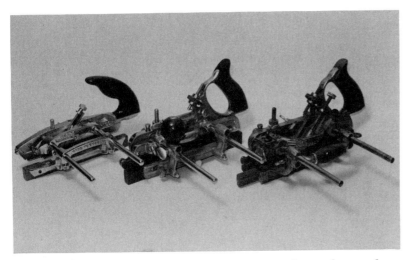

Illus. 6-1. In this chapter, I cover three universal combination planes. Shown from left to right, they are the Record 045C, the Stanley #45, and the Stanley #55 planes. The Record 045C is still being produced. The Stanley #45 is not being produced anymore, but the Clifton Multi-Plane is similar to it and is still being made. The Stanley #55 is not being produced at present, but used ones are still fairly easy to find on the used tool market.

Record Multi-Plane have similar capabilities. The Stanley #55 can make a wider variety of mouldings, because the runner on the sliding section can be adjusted vertically. In the first part of this chapter, I will cover the procedures common to all three planes. On pages 96–105, I discuss the additional capabilities of the Stanley #55.

Universal combination planes do have some limitations. The most obvious is the amount of setup time needed to get the plane ready for each different job. For example, if you make many tongue-and-groove joints, you would be better off getting a set of match planes, because they are ready for use whenever you need them. If you only occasionally need to make a tongue-and-groove joint, then the extra setup time involved in getting the universal combination plane ready is not much of a problem.

The second drawback of the universal combination plane is not as obvious. Because the plane uses runners instead of a solid sole, there is nothing pressing down on the wood directly in front of the cutter. This becomes a problem mostly when mouldings are being cut. A traditional moulding plane has a wood sole that is shaped to fit the moulding. This helps to prevent tear-out. Tear-out will be more of a problem with a universal combination plane than with a traditional moulding plane. For this reason, it is best to select the wood carefully; use straight-grained boards and avoid highly figured wood. Even with these drawbacks, a universal combination plane can be a valuable addition to your tools, particularly if you don't

have a large collection of specialty planes to perform these jobs.

Setup and Adjustment

All of the universal combination planes are similar in many respects, so some general directions will apply to all of them. The Stanley #55 has additional capabilities that are discussed on pages 96–105. In the directions that follow, when I refer to the right or left side of the plane, I am assuming that the plane is being held in its normal working position, with the user viewing it from above.

The Record 045C is the same plow/combination plane described in Chapter 4. To use it as a universal combination plane, you must install the conversion kit K050C (Illus. 6-2). The parts of the 045C are labelled in Illus. 6-3. To install the conversion kit, remove the cutter clamp and replace it with the sliding section from the kit. This sliding section includes a second sole runner and a second nicker. The kit also includes a beading stop. This accessory is discussed in the section on beadings.

To install a cutter in the 045C plane, loosen the cutter clamp nut. Place the cutter between the sliding section and the main stock. The cutter fits into grooves milled in the side of the sliding section and the main stock. Align the notch in the cutter with the collar on the adjusting nut. Turn the adjusting nut to make the initial adjustment of

Illus. 6-2. The conversion kit K050C includes this sliding section, which replaces the standard cutter clamp. It adds a second sole runner and a second nicker to the Record 045C plane.

the cutter. Now, tighten the cutter clamp nut. To readjust the cutter, slightly loosen the cutter clamp nut and turn the adjusting nut up or down.

The fence slides onto the two arms of the plane and is held in place by two knurled screws. As supplied from the factory, there is no wooden face on the fence. Adding a shop-made wooden face to the fence will make the plane more stable and avoid scratches on the face of the work. The fence face should be made from a hard wood. It must have cutouts in the same places as the metal fence, to provide clearance for the runner and the cutter (Illus. 6-4).

The depth stop slides up and down in a hole in the main stock of the plane. To adjust it, twist the knurled rod counterclockwise. Slide the rod up or down to the proper position and then twist the knurled rod clockwise to lock the adjustment.

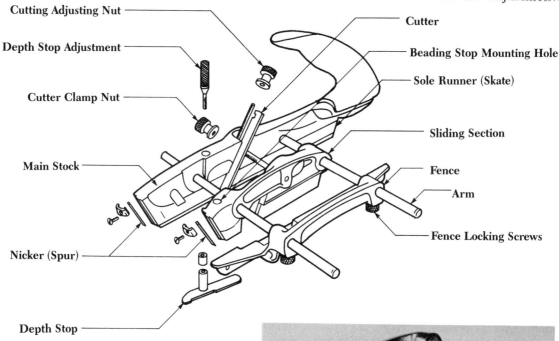

Cutting Adjusting Nut

Depth Stop Adjustment

Cutter Clamp Nut

Main Stock

Nicker (Spur)

Depth Stop

Cutter

Beading Stop Mounting Hole

Sole Runner (Skate)

Sliding Section

Fence

Arm

Fence Locking Screws

Illus. 6-3. Parts of the Record 045C plane.

Illus. 6-4. The Record 045C fence slides onto the two arms of the plane and is held in place by two knurled screws. As supplied from the factory, there is no wooden face on the fence. Adding a shop-made wooden face to the fence will make the plane more stable and avoid scratches on the face of the work.

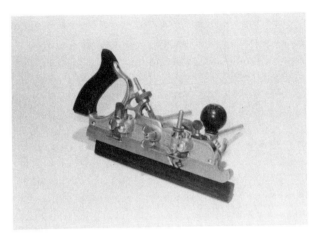

Illus. 6-5. The Record Multi-Plane and the Stanley #45 plane are very similar in appearance and operation. The setup procedures are the same for both.

This depth stop is unique in its operation. Tightening the knurled rod compresses a nylon bushing. This causes it to expand inside the hole in the main stock, locking the depth stop.

The setup procedures for the Record Multi-Plane and the Stanley #45 are the same (Illus. 6-5). The Stanley #55 also shares many of the same features, so the same basic setup procedures also apply to the #55. The parts for the Stanley #45 and the Record Multi-Plane are given in Illus. 6-6.

To install one of the cutters in the main stock of the plane, loosen the cutter bolt wing nut on the right side of the plane. This will cause the tapered cutter bolt to move out of the left side of the plane.

Now, place the desired cutter on the bed of the

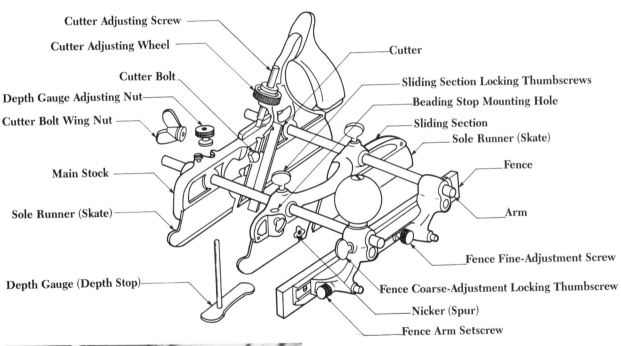

Cutter Adjusting Screw

Cutter Adjusting Wheel

Cutter Bolt

Depth Gauge Adjusting Nut

Cutter Bolt Wing Nut

Main Stock

Sole Runner (Skate)

Depth Gauge (Depth Stop)

Cutter

Sliding Section Locking Thumbscrews

Beading Stop Mounting Hole

Sliding Section

Sole Runner (Skate)

Fence

Arm

Fence Fine-Adjustment Screw

Fence Coarse-Adjustment Locking Thumbscrew

Nicker (Spur)

Fence Arm Setscrew

Illus. 6-6. Parts of the Stanley #45 plane and the Multi-Plane.

Illus. 6-7. The procedure for installing a cutter in the main stock of a #45, #55, or Multi-Plane is the same. Loosen the cutter bolt wing nut on the right side of the plane. Place the cutter on the bed of the plane and slide it to the right until it sits under the cutter bolt. Then align the notch on the top of the cutter with the pin on the top of the cutter adjusting screw, and tighten the wing nut on the cutter bolt.

plane and slide it to the right until it sits under the cutter bolt. As you slide the cutter in place, you must also line up the notch on the top of the cutter with the pin on the top of the cutter adjusting screw (Illus. 6-7).

Next, tighten the wing nut on the cutter bolt. To adjust the cutting depth, loosen the wing nut about one-half turn, and then turn the cutter adjusting wheel to raise or lower the cutter. When the adjustment is complete, turn the adjusting wheel clockwise to remove all of the slack and then tighten the wing nut on the cutter bolt.

Cutters that are less than ¼ inch wide will not have a notch for the pin in the cutter adjusting screw. When you install these cutters, butt their ends up against the pin. To make an adjustment, hold the cutter against the pin by applying pressure with one finger while turning the adjusting wheel with the other hand. This method is as accurate as the screw adjustment, even though the cutter doesn't have a notch.

Next, install the sliding section. When you are using some of the narrowest cutters, you will not use the sliding section. However, for most work, it is required. If the arms are not already in place, put them through the holes in the main stock and tighten the setscrews. For most work, the arms are placed with their ends flush with the right side of the main stock. In some cases, it is desirable to have a fence on the right side. In that case, extend the arms sufficiently past the right side of the plane to attach the fence.

Now, align the holes in the sliding section with the arms and slide the sliding section into position. The exact placement of the sliding section depends on the cutter being used and the job at hand. For now, simply line up the outside edge of the runner with the left edge of the cutter. Tighten the thumbscrews to secure the sliding section.

The fence is used for most work. There are two sets of holes in the fence that can be used to attach it to the arms. For most jobs, use the upper holes. The lower holes can be used when it is desirable to raise the fence. Make the rough fence adjustment by sliding the fence along the arms and then tightening the thumbscrews. Fine adjustments

can be made by loosening the fence arm setscrew and turning the fence adjusting screw (Illus. 6-8). After completing the adjustment, retighten the fence arm setscrew.

The depth of cut is set by loosening the setscrew and turning the depth gauge nut. This raises or lowers the adjustable depth gauge (Illus. 6-9). There is an additional depth stop towards the rear of the main stock on the right side. This is the position where the slitting cutter can be installed. The main purpose of this stop is to regulate the depth of the slitting cutter, but it can also be used as an additional depth stop for other tasks. If you set it level with the adjustable depth gauge, it will support the rear of the plane when you reach the desired depth.

There is another depth gauge that can be attached to the left side of the sliding section. It fits into the hole right in front of the front arm thumbscrew. This depth gauge is primarily used when making dadoes, because the main depth gauge is blocked by the board clamped to the work to guide the cut. You can also use this depth gauge to give additional support to prevent the plane from cutting deeper on the left side when you reach the depth stop.

There are two other attachments that are used in special situations: the cam rest and the beading stop. The cam rest slides onto the front arm between the fence and the sliding section (Illus. 6-10). Its purpose is to support the arm when the fence is set at a distance from the main stock. This prevents the plane from rocking. As the cut progresses, the cam rest must be rotated to keep the arms level.

The beading stop is used to guide the cut when making a bead next to a tongue. In this case, the tongue interferes with the normal operation of the fence, so the beading stop is used as a small fence that rides above the tongue on the edge of the board. It fits into the hole in front of the front arm thumbscrew in the sliding section. The use of these two attachments will be covered in more detail in later sections.

Universal combination planes can be fitted with a variety of different cutters. The Record 045C plane is only supplied with one cutter as standard equipment. The other cutters are all optional. There are two sets of cutters available. The first set contains straight plow cutters ranging in width from ⅛ to ½ inch. These are the cutters used for making grooves, dadoes, and rabbets. The second set includes two larger plow cutters, five beading cutters, and a tongue cutter. There are 12 other cutters that are sold individually.

The Stanley #45 plane and the Record Multi-Plane came with a set of cutters as standard equipment. Additional cutters were optional. The Clifton reproduction of the Multi-Plane comes with 13 standard cutters. An optional cutter set is available with 16 additional cutters. Illus. 6-11 shows the types of cutters available.

Illus. 6-8. The fence is used to guide the plane. Make the rough fence adjustment by sliding the fence along the arms and then tightening the thumbscrews. Fine adjustments can be made by loosening the fence arm setscrew and turning the fence adjusting screw.

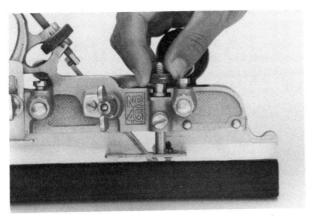

Illus. 6-9. The depth of cut is set by loosening the setscrew and turning the depth gauge nut. This raises or lowers the adjustable depth gauge.

Illus. 6-10. The cam rest slides onto the front arm between the fence and the sliding section. Its purpose is to support the arm when the fence is set at a distance from the main stock. This prevents the plane from rocking.

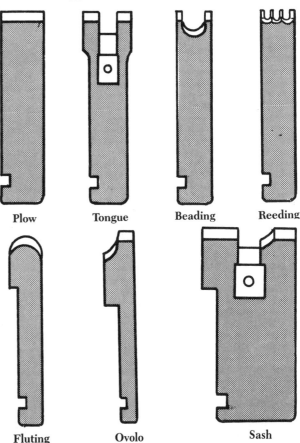

Plow　　Tongue　　Beading　　Reeding

Fluting　　Ovolo　　Sash

Illus. 6-11. Universal combination planes can be fitted with a variety of different cutters. Virtually all the cutters shown in this illustration will fit the three universal combination planes described in this chapter. The only exception is the ovolo cutter, which is specifically made for the Multi-Plane. Each type of cutter is available in a range of sizes.

There are two keys to successfully using a universal combination plane. First, the cutters must be honed to a keen edge. Second, you must make a very fine cut. These two rules are particularly important when you are using the larger cutters such as the tongue or the sash cutters. If these cutters are not razor-sharp, the plane will be so hard to push it will stop you completely. If you attempt to take a cut that is too rank, the plane will choke rapidly.

The cutters come from the factory ground to the correct 35-degree angle, but they are not honed. Before using them, hone them with a fine stone. The cutters that have square cutting edges are simple to hone. Just follow the directions in Chapter 2. Cutters that have curved profiles require the use of slipstones. A slipstone is a small whetstone that is rounded or tapered. Slipstones come in a variety of shapes. You can get a set of ceramic slipstones called ceramic files that can be used in most situations.

If there are straight edges on the cutter, sharpen them first on a flat stone, and then use the slipstone to sharpen the curved sections. Hold the cutter on the edge of the bench with its cutting edge extended over the edge or place it in a vise. For some cutters, such as beading cutters, it is easier to place the slipstone in a vise padded with wood blocks and move the cutter (Illus. 6-12). Place the slipstone on the cutting edge and adjust the angle that you hold the stone at until it matches the angle ground at the factory. It is best not to create a secondary bevel. If you placed the slipstone in a vise, push the cutter over the stone. If you have the cutter in the vise, push the slipstone into the cutter. Push repeatedly until the grinding marks on the cutting edge have been polished out. Now, back off the wire edge by placing the back of the cutter flat on a whetstone and rubbing it for several strokes. If necessary, use the slipstone again to remove the wire edge from the bevel side.

The three universal combination planes described in this chapter incorporate nickers to score a shoulder line when cross-grain cuts are being made. The nickers on the Record 045C are positioned at the front of the runners. They are

Illus. 6-12. An easy way to sharpen beading cutters is to clamp a slipstone that matches the curvature of the cutter in a vise padded with wood blocks. Don't tighten the vise too much or you can break the stone. With this setup, the sharpening procedure is the same as if you were sharpening a straight cutter on a flat stone. For other cutters, it may be easier to clamp the cutter in the vise and use a variety of different-shaped ceramic files. Be careful to maintain the original profile of the cutter when you are sharpening. No secondary bevel is used on the cutters that have curves. You can add a secondary bevel to the straight cutters.

clamped in position with a screw (Illus. 6-13). The nickers on the Stanley #45 and the Record Multi-Plane are located on the side of the runners just in front of the cutter. They have three positions (Illus. 6-14). Only one is sharpened at the factory. The other two positions should be kept as spares for the time when, after many sharpenings, the original nicker is too short. The nickers on the #55 plane are also located on the side of the runners. They only have one cutting edge, but they can be adjusted up and down to compensate for wear (Illus. 6-15).

To be effective, the nickers should be honed. The Record 045C nickers are large enough to grab with your fingers and sharpen on a whetstone. Just follow the original angles ground at the factory. The nickers on the other planes are so small that it is hard to use your fingers to hold them. You can grab them with a pair of needle-nose pliers, and then hone their edges on the side of a flat whetstone.

Illus. 6-13. The nickers on the Record 045C plane are clamped to the front of the sole runner.

Illus. 6-14. The nickers on the Stanley #45 plane and Multi-Plane are the cloverleaf type. They are mounted on the side of the runners, just ahead of the mouth.

Illus. 6-15. The Stanley #55 plane uses this type of nicker.

Using a Universal Combination Plane

The universal combination plane will perform all of the jobs done by a rabbet plane, a fillister, a plow plane, and a dado plane. I will describe how to set up and use the universal combination plane for these applications first, and then I will explore the additional capabilities of the universal combination plane (Illus. 6-16). All of the planes described in this chapter are capable of making tongue-and-groove joints, beading, reeding, fluting, and making sash. The Stanley #55 has additional capabilities that are covered in the next section.

Cutting Rabbets

To cut a rabbet using a universal plane, install a plow cutter in the main stock (Illus. 6-17). The width of the cutter should be greater than the desired width of the rabbet. The runner position on the Record 045C plane is fixed at the outside edge of the cutter. This means that when making rabbets, the runner on the sliding section will be off the work. Therefore, you must be careful not to let the plane tip as you work, or the rabbet will slope to the outside. The other planes have an adjustable sliding section. This enables you to position the runner to provide better support for the plane.

Set the runner on the sliding section so that it will ride ⅛ to ¼ inch in from the edge of the board. The exact dimension is not critical. For small rabbets, the runner can be closer to the edge. For large ones, it can be farther from the edge.

Attach the fence. You must use the upper set of arm holes on the #45 and #55 planes and the Multi-Plane, because the fence has to slide under the cutter. Measure from the face of the fence to the right side of the main-stock runner to determine the width of the rabbet. When the fence is correctly positioned, tighten the thumbscrews on it. Fine adjustments in the fence position can be made using the fence adjusting screw. Set the adjustable depth gauge to control the depth of the rabbet.

Place the board on the bench with the face to be

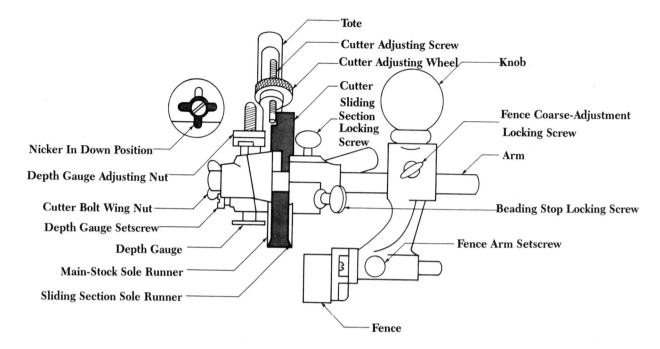

Illus. 6-16. *Parts of the Multi-Plane, as viewed from the front. Refer to this illustration when studying the setup drawings that follow. The setups for the Stanley #45 and #55 planes are very similar. The setups for the Record 045C plane are basically the same; refer to the exploded view of the 045C plane (Illus. 6-4) and compare its part locations with this drawing.*

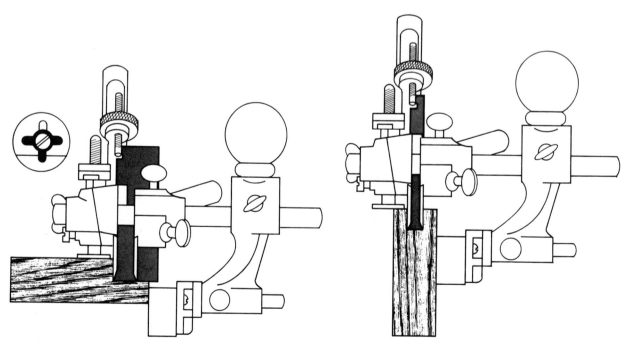

Illus. 6-17. *A universal combination plane set up to cut rabbets.*

Illus. 6-18. *A universal combination plane set up to cut grooves.*

rabbeted up. The edge of the board must overhang the edge of the bench slightly, because the fence will project below the board. Clamp the board or use bench stops to hold it in position. You can now use the plane exactly as described for the fillister in Chapter 4. For rabbets cut with the grain, the nicker is not used. When making a rabbet across the grain, lower the nicker.

Cutting Grooves

Grooves are made using the plow cutters (Illus. 6-18). You must choose a cutter that is the exact width of the desired groove. If a nonstandard-size groove is needed, it is possible to use a smaller cutter and make two overlapping grooves.

Install the cutter in the main stock. Note that the ⅛-inch cutter does not have a notch for the pin on the cutter adjusting screw. When using this cutter, butt the end of the cutter against the pin and make the adjustments as described previously.

Next, install the sliding section. The runner on the Record 045C plane is fixed in its correct position. On the other planes, slide the sliding section over until the left side of the runner is flush with the left edge of the cutter. Then tighten the thumbscrews. Note that when you are using cutters smaller than ¼ inch, you will not use the sliding section.

Grooves can be cut in the face or edge of the board. In both cases, the procedure is similar. Set the fence to regulate the position of the groove and set the depth gauge to control the depth of the groove.

When making a groove on the face of a board, it may be helpful to use the cam rest. This will only be needed when the groove is several inches away from the edge. To use the cam rest, slide it onto the front arm after the sliding section is in place but before you install the fence. Place the plane onto the work and rotate the cam until it touches the face of the board. Now, begin plowing the groove. After a few strokes, you must rotate the cam slightly to lower the arm position. Keep rotating the cam as you progress downwards.

The procedure for plowing the groove is exactly the same as described in Chapter 4 for the plow plane.

Cutting Dadoes

To cut a dado, select a plow cutter that is the correct width and install it in the main stock. Place the sliding section on the arms and slide it into position (Illus. 6-19). The outside edge of the runner should line up exactly with the edge of the cutter.

Lower both of the nickers to scribe the shoulders of the dado. The fence is not used. Instead, clamp a board to the work to guide the plane. The right side of the main-stock runner should ride against the guide board. Raise the adjustable depth gauge up so that it doesn't interfere with the guide board. Attach the extra depth gauge to the left side of the plane. It fits in a hole just in

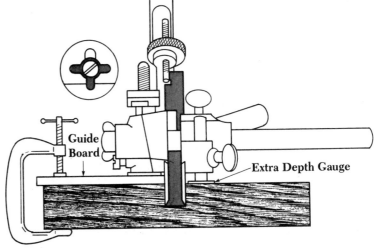

Illus. 6-19. A universal combination plane set up to cut dadoes.

Guide Board

Extra Depth Gauge

front of the thumbscrew at the front of the sliding section. Set this depth gauge to control the depth of the dado.

The procedure for using the plane is the same as that for using a plow plane to cut a dado given in Chapter 4.

Cutting Tongue-and-Grooves

The universal plane can be used as a matching plane to cut tongue-and-grooves. Two separate setups are required, one to cut the tongue and the other to cut the groove. The setup for the groove is made exactly as given above in the section on grooves (Illus. 6-20).

To make the tongue, install one of the tongue cutters in the plane (Illus. 6-21). There are two cutters available; one makes a ¼-inch-wide tongue, the other makes a ³⁄₁₆-inch-wide tongue. As shown in Illus. 6-21, there is a small part attached with a screw in the middle of the groove opening. This is the depth gauge. The standard depth gauges on the plane will not work when making a tongue, so the depth of the cut is regulated by the position of the depth gauge on the cutter. You can loosen the screw and slide the depth gauge up or down. It will stop the cut when it contacts the end of the tongue.

Install the sliding section and position it so that it will ride slightly past the side of the tongue. Install the fence next. You must use the upper set of arm holes, because the fence has to slide under a portion of the cutter. Adjust the fence to locate the tongue. It can be centered or placed off to one side, depending on the application.

Place the board edge-up in a wedge stop on top of the bench, or put it in a vise. Use pegs on the front of the bench to support long boards. Short boards can be worked all at once. Longer boards can be worked down in sections. When working down a long board, start at the toe end of the board and work down a two- or three-foot section. Then step rearwards and work down another section. After the entire length has been worked down in this manner, take two or three passes along the entire length of the board.

Set the cutter for a fine cut. The work will go faster and turn out better if a fine cut is used. You

Illus. 6-20. Making the groove for a tongue-and-groove joint using the Record 045C plane.

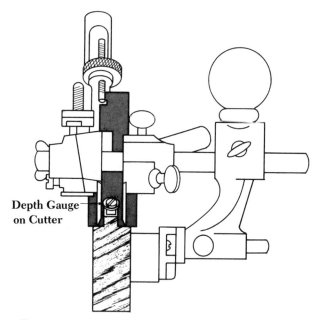

Depth Gauge on Cutter

Illus. 6-21. A universal combination plane set up to cut a tongue.

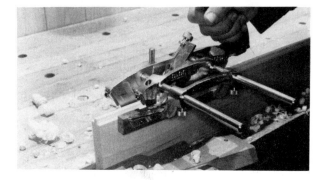

Illus. 6-22. Making the tongue of a tongue-and-groove joint using the Record 045C plane. Normally, you should hold on to the front arm of the plane with your other hand. I moved my hand for this photograph so you can see the plane better.

will need to take about 20 passes to work down an average-size tongue, but you can do this quickly when the plane is adjusted properly (Illus. 6-22). Knots and abrupt changes in grain can cause chipped sections in the tongue, but this is not a major problem because the tongue will be hidden by the matching groove.

After you have finished a forward stroke, lift the heel of the plane so that the cutter does not drag on the wood as you pull the plane rearwards. Let the curved section of the runners at the front ride on the work as you pull the plane back. This will keep the plane in position for the next forward stroke. If you lift the plane completely off the work, the process is much slower and you run the risk of damaging the tongue as you reposition the plane at the beginning of the next stroke.

Beading

You will probably use the beading cutters more than any other moulding cutter. Beads are a frequently used traditional decoration. Beads are often used in conjunction with a tongue-and-groove joint to hide the gap between the boards. If you make antique reproduction furniture, the beading capabilities of the universal plane are invaluable.

The small grooves that define the edges of the bead are called *quirks*. When a bead is made on the edge of a board, it only has one quirk. A center bead has two quirks. The beading cutter will also make an *astragal*. An astragal has a flat fillet instead of a quirk (Illus. 6-23).

Using Beads on a Matched Board Always make the bead on the tongue edge of the board. Beading the grooved edge would weaken the joint.

Install the beading cutter in the main stock of the plane. There are several sizes of beading cutters that come with the plane. They range from ⅛ to ½ inch. Larger beading cutters are optional. The cutters are designed so that when seated properly in the bed, the right edge of the cutter will be flush with the right side of the main-stock runner (Illus. 6-24).

The standard fence will not regulate the position of the bead accurately enough, because the

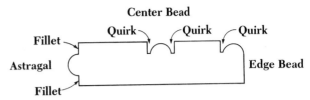

Illus. 6-23. *The astragal, center bead, and edge bead are all made with the same beading cutter.*

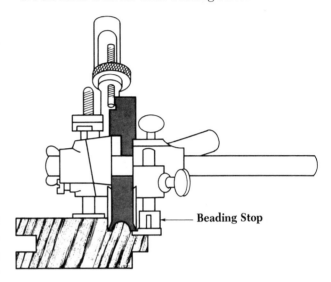

Illus. 6-24. *A universal combination plane set up to bead matched boards.*

tongue is in the way. To guide the cut, install the beading stop to the sliding section. It will fit in the same hole as is used for the extra depth gauge. There is a lip on the edge of the beading stop. This should fit against the bottom of the sliding section runner (Illus. 6-25). It is not necessary to use the fence, because the beading stop will guide the plane (Illus. 6-26). If you like, you can install the fence so the front knob on the Stanley #45 plane or the Multi-Plane can be used to help hold the plane (Illus. 6-27). Slide the fence over until it just touches the end of the tongue.

The position of the beading stop is fixed on the Record 045C plane. On the other planes, the beading stop position is controlled by adjusting the position of the sliding section. The bead position is correct when the side of the bead is fully rounded and there is no trace of the flat bottom of the outside quirk on the edge of the board. Make test cuts on scrap to determine that the stop is correctly adjusted. The depth of the bead is con-

Illus. 6-25. The beading stop is used to guide the cut when you are beading matched boards. It will fit in the same hole as is used for the extra depth gauge. There is a lip on the edge of the beading stop. This should fit against the bottom of the sliding section runner.

Illus. 6-26. Beading a matched board using the Record 045C plane. Note that the fence is not used. The cut is guided by the beading stop. You can see the knurled handle of the beading stop extending from the top of the sliding section.

Illus. 6-27. Beading a matched board using the #45 plane. Although the beading stop is guiding the cut, the fence has been installed so that the front knob can be used.

trolled with the adjustable depth gauge. It is a good idea to work the bead down slightly below the surface of the board. That way, you can smooth the surface of the board later with a smooth plane without flattening the top of the bead.

Place the board face-up on the bench and clamp it or use bench stops to hold it in position. You can work the entire length of a short board all at once. For long boards, start at the toe end and work down until you almost get to the depth stop. Then step back and work down another short section. When you have worked down the entire board in this manner, make several full-length strokes by walking with the plane along the entire length of the board. When the depth stop rides on the face of the board along its entire length, you can stop. At the end of each forward stroke, raise the heel of the plane but leave the curved section of the runner in the quirk.

Now, pull the plane back on the return stroke. Before starting the next forward stroke, lower the plane so that the runner is fully in the quirk and the beading stop is against the edge. Be careful as you position the plane for each stroke, because a small misalignment will show up as a dip in the side of the bead.

Using Beads on Boards Without Tongues The procedure for making a bead on the edge of a board that does not have a tongue is similar, except that the fence is used and the beading stop is not. The fence controls the position of the bead. Usually, the bead is positioned so that none of the flat bottom of the outside quirk is formed; this produces a smoothly rounded edge on the board.

If the board will be butted up against another board, then you can make an astragal. Position the fence so that a fillet is formed on the edge. When the boards are butted together, the edge of the other board against the fillet will make the joint look like a center bead.

A *return bead* is sometimes used when two boards are joined at a corner (Illus. 6-28). The return bead requires two steps. First, set up the plane to make a bead on the front edge of the board. Offset the bead so that the fillet on the face side is very small. Next, set up the plane to make a

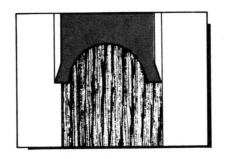

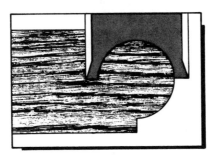

Illus. 6-28. A return bead can be used when two boards are joined at a corner. The return bead requires two steps. First, as shown in the top box, set up the plane to make a bead on the front edge of the board. Offset the bead so that the fillet on the face side is very small. Second, as shown in the bottom box, set up the plane to make a bead on the face of the board. Adjust the position of the fence until the result is a fully rounded bead.

bead on the face of the board. Adjust the position of the fence until the result is a fully rounded bead. It is advisable to check the setups on a piece of scrap before working the project boards.

When the bead is located away from the edge of the board, it is called a *center bead*. When a universal plane is used to make a center bead, the runners can bind against the sides of the quirks, unless they are adjusted precisely. The best way to get a precise adjustment is to first make a bead on a scrap board. After you have worked down a little, loosen the thumbscrews on the sliding runner and let the runners settle down into the

quirks. Now, retighten the thumbscrews and finish the bead. Loosen the thumbscrews again and let the runners slide together until they fit perfectly in the quirks. Next, tighten the thumbscrews. You are ready to start the beads on the actual project boards.

Use the fence to guide the plane as you make center beads. If the bead is more than a few inches away from the edge, you should use the cam rest to help keep the fence arms level. Place the cam rest on the front arm between the sliding section and the fence (Illus. 6-29). Adjust it so that it is resting on the face of the board as you begin to cut

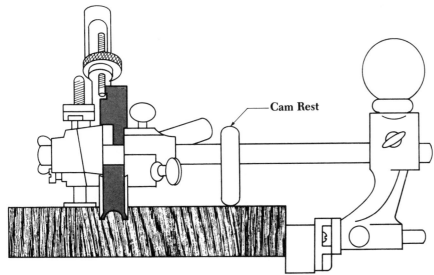

Cam Rest

Illus. 6-29. A universal combination plane set up to cut a center bead.

the bead. After each stroke, rotate the cam slightly to lower the arm. If you tighten the set-screw until it is snug but not extremely tight, you can rotate the cam without loosening the screw. If the cam slips during use, then you will need to tighten the screw more.

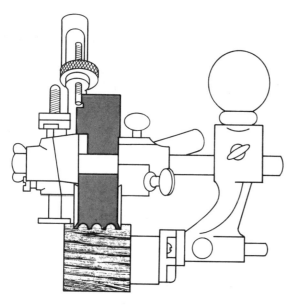

Illus. 6-30. A universal combination plane set up for reeding using a reeding cutter.

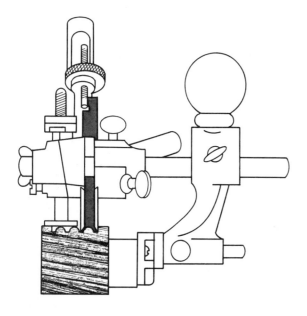

Illus. 6-31. A universal combination plane set up for reeding using a beading cutter.

Reeding

A reed is a series of beads cut side by side. There are optional reeding cutters that cut all of the beads at once, or you can use a beading cutter and make multiple passes.

A reeding cutter works just like a beading cutter. Install a reeding cutter in the plane and then follow the directions given for center-beading (Illus. 6-30).

To use a single beading cutter for reeding, set up the plane as described for center-beading. Adjust the fence to position the bead that is the farthest away from the edge, and then cut the bead. Now, loosen the fence thumbscrews and slide the fence over until the runner on the main stock is lined up with the left quirk of the first bead. Tighten the thumbscrews and cut the next bead. Continue in this manner until the desired number of beads have been cut (Illus. 6-31).

Fluting

Fluting is another decorative cut that is often used when making antique reproductions. Fluting is frequently used as a decoration on table legs. The fluting cutters range in size from ³⁄₁₆ to ¾ inch. They are designed so that the main-stock runner will line up close to the middle of the cutter rather than flush with the edge, as is the case with the beading cutters. The sliding section is not used with fluting cutters. The position of the flute is regulated with the fence, and the depth is set with the depth stop (Illus. 6-32).

The procedure for cutting the flutes is similar to the procedure already described for cutting beads. If several flutes are to be cut side by side, start with the one farthest from the edge and work progressively towards the edge.

Cutting Ovolos

Most edge mouldings cannot be made without the vertically adjustable sole runner of the #55 plane, but the Multi-Plane does come with specially designed ovolo cutters to allow you to make this one type of edge moulding. The ovolo cutters have a notch cut out in their sides, so that the curved portion of the cutter is on the outside of the main-

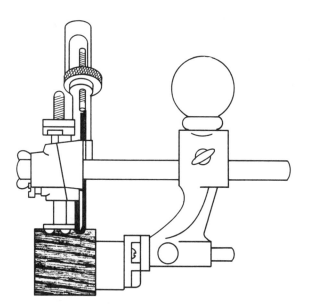

Illus. 6-32. A universal combination plane set up for fluting.

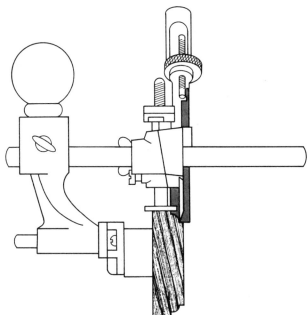

Illus. 6-33. A universal combination plane set up to cut an ovolo.

stock sole runner. This cutter doesn't work well in the Record 045C plane, because the throat is not quite deep enough and the depth stop will interfere with the cutter.

To set up the plane to make an ovolo, remove the sliding section; it is not used with this cutter. Next, install the cutter. To use the widest ovolo cutter, it may be necessary to remove the front adjustable depth gauge. In that case, use the rear depth gauge to control the depth of cut. The cut can be made with the plane riding on either the face or the edge of the board. If the board is small enough to allow you to clamp it vertically in the vise, it is best to make the cut with the plane riding on the edge of the board. This allows you to position the fence as shown in Illus. 6-33.

When cutting an ovolo, there is a tendency for the plane to wander away from the edge, because the curvature of the cutter forces it away from the work. You can counteract this by placing the fence on the opposite side of the board. To move the fence to the opposite side of the plane, loosen the two screws that secure the arms to the main stock and slide the arms through the main stock so that they project from the other side. Now, turn the fence around and slide it onto the arms. This will place the knob at the rear of the plane, but you can simply hold on to the front arm instead.

If the size of the board makes this method impossible, you can cut the ovolo on the face of the board with the fence in the usual position. Apply extra side pressure to the plane to keep the fence securely against the edge.

Using the Sash Cutter

The sash cutter makes the universal combination plane capable of performing the work of a sash plane. Sash planes are a special type of moulding plane used to make windows. In a traditional wooden window, the small panes of glass are held in sash, a framework made of stiles and rails and divided by sash bars. Sash bars can also be called muntins. The shape of these sash bars is rather complex and difficult to make without specialized tools. The sash plane is designed to make the rabbet for the glass and the moulded edge in a single step. Sash planes are no longer in production, but the sash cutter for the universal combination planes performs the same job. While you may not need to make windows for a house, the sash cutter can still be useful for making glazed doors for cabinets.

Early sash makers made the rabbet and the

moulding in separate steps. Later, sash planes were developed that combined a rabbet plane with a moulding plane. The sash cutter for the universal combination planes is also designed to cut the rabbet and the moulding in a single operation.

Begin by installing the sash cutter in the plane. The same sash cutter will cut a rabbet and make a moulded edge on both the sash bars and the stiles and rails of a window or a glazed door. The setup is similar to that described for making a tongue. Like the tongue cutter, the sash cutter has a built-in depth stop. To set the depth, loosen the screw and slide the stop up or down on the cutter. Install the cutter in the main stock of the plane. Adjust the sliding section so that the runner will rest on the flat fillet of the moulding near the outside edge. Set the fence so that a little bit of the cutter projects past the outside edge of the board.

Start by working the edges of the stiles and rails that form the frame of the window. If you like, you can cut the moulding on long boards, and then cut the parts to length. Since the moulded edge is highly visible, you should use straight-grained lumber that is knot-free, to avoid chipped areas.

Place the board edge-up in a vise; if the board is long, support the far end of it with a peg on the front of the bench. Place the plane on the work with the fence resting against the face of the board. Work down the moulding using the same procedure described for the tongue cutter. If you are making a window with a single piece of glass, then you won't need any sash bars. If smaller, individual panes of glass will be used, then you will need to make sash bars next.

The easiest way for a novice to make a sash bar is to use a wide board that can be easily clamped to the bench and saw the moulded section off after he or she has finished planing. Place the board on the bench with one of its faces up. Plane down to the depth stop. Then turn the board over and plane down the other side (Illus. 6-34). After the planing is done, you can saw through the tail of the sash bar to remove it from the wide board. You can then plane another sash bar out of the same board.

Old-time sash makers sometimes worked sash bars in pairs. If you would like to try this method,

cut a piece of wood that is twice as wide as the finished sash bar. Place it face-up on the bench and butt the end of the board against a bench stop. Using the same setup as described above, plane down the first edge of the board. Now, turn the board around and plane the other edge. Next, turn the board over and repeat the process (Illus. 6-35).

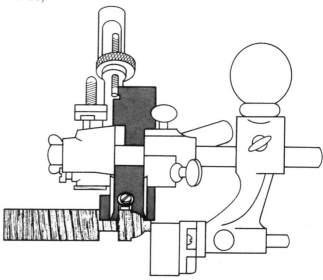

Illus. 6-34. A universal combination plane set up to make sash bars. Cut the tail of the sash bar free with a saw after you have finished planing.

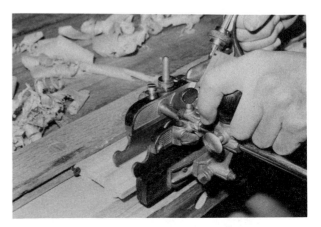

Illus. 6-35. Old-time sash makers sometimes worked sash bars in pairs. If you would like to try this method, cut a piece of wood that is twice as wide as the finished sash bar. Here I am using a simple sticking board to hold the work. It is simply a board with a groove in its edge and a screwhead that projects from the groove that acts as a stop.

Illus. 6-36. The Stanley #45 plane, the Multi-Plane, and the Stanley #55 plane have the capability to be used as a slitter.

After the planing was done, old-time sash makers used a specialized tool called a slitter to cut the two sash bars apart. The slitter is a sharp blade mounted in a stock with an adjustable fence. The fence is set for the length of the tail of one sash bar. The blade is used to slit halfway through from each side. When you have made a slit on both sides, you can snap the sash bars apart. The Stanley #45 plane, the Multi-Plane, and the Stanley #55 plane have the capability to be used as a slitter (Illus. 6-36).

To use the plane as a slitter, remove the sash cutter and install the slitter on the main stock of the plane. Use the fence to position the cutter so that it will cut down the centerline between the two sash bars. Set the cutter stop for one-half the thickness of the tail of the sash bar. Push the plane the full length of the work. Make additional passes until the stop hits. Then turn the board over and repeat the procedure. As the two slits meet, the bars will snap apart. The edge left by the cutter may be slightly irregular. You can square it up with a bench plane.

The next step in making a sash is to cut the parts to length and make the joints. Sash joinery can be complex. For complete details on sash joints, refer to my book *Wood Joiner's Handbook*.

The glass can be held in place with glazing putty or wooden fixing beads. Glazing putty is usually used on exterior windows where weather resistance is more important than appearance. For glazed cabinet doors, where appearance is important, wooden fixing beads are preferable. You can make the fixing bead using the universal plane.

To make a fixing bead, install the ½-inch beading cutter in the main stock of the plane. Install the sliding section and align it with the edge of the cutter. Install the fence using the upper set of arm holes. Slide the fence over until it covers half of the cutter. The moulding is cut from a piece of ⅜-inch-thick stock. The board should be wide enough to allow it to be clamped to the bench.

Now, cut the moulding as shown in Illus. 6-37. You can use a ripsaw to cut the moulding from the edge of the board. Leave some extra wood between the cut and the quirk. After the moulding has been separated from the board, plane off this extra wood with a smooth plane. This will give the moulding a clean edge.

Instead of using a saw to remove the moulding, you can use a ⅛-inch plow cutter in the plane. Adjust the fence so that the edge of the cut is aligned with the end of the quirk. Turn the board over and plane a groove in the back of the board. When the groove meets the quirk, the moulding will fall free. This method leaves a smooth edge on the moulding; a small amount of cleanup with a

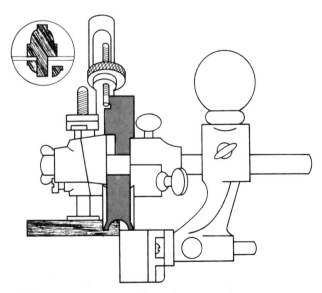

Illus. 6-37. A universal combination plane set up to make a fixing bead. The fixing bead can be used to hold the glass in the rabbet on the sash bars.

block plane may be necessary to remove the thin ridge left where the two cuts met.

Install the moulding after the glass has been placed in the frame. Where the fixing beads meet at the corners, they should be mitred. Use small brads to secure the fixing bead.

Using the Stanley #55 Plane

The Stanley #55 plane is capable of performing more jobs than any of the other universal combination planes (Illus. 6-38). In many respects, it is similar to the Stanley #45 plane. The feature that distinguishes the #55 is a vertical adjustment on the sliding section runner (Illus. 6-39). The #55 can do all of the jobs described in the previous sections in this chapter. The directions given in this chapter also apply to the #55, assuming that the sliding section runner is adjusted to the same level as the main-stock runner.

If you don't need the additional capabilities of the #55, you will be better off using one of the other planes. The vertical adjustment of the runner makes it more difficult to set up the plane. If the sliding section runner is not set to the correct level, it can affect the way the plane cuts.

Because the Stanley #55 has a vertical adjustment for the sliding section runner, it can be used to cut edge mouldings that cannot be cut with the other planes (Illus. 6-40). Now that traditional moulding planes are difficult to find, the Stanley #55 plane can be very useful to any woodworker who wants to duplicate period mouldings. It is particularly useful for restorers who may need to duplicate a small section of moulding to match existing pieces. Even though there may be considerable setup time involved in getting the #55 plane ready to make a duplicate moulding, it is worthwhile.

The #55 plane differs from the #45 plane in several other respects. Illus. 6-41 shows an exploded view of the #55 plane. Note that there is a small third runner called the *auxiliary center bottom*. Like the runner on the sliding section, this auxiliary center bottom can be adjusted vertically.

Illus. 6-38. The Stanley #55 plane is capable of performing more jobs than any of the other universal combination planes.

Illus. 6-39. The feature that distinguishes the Stanley #55 plane from the other planes is a vertical adjustment on the sliding section runner. In this photograph, the sliding section has been removed from the plane to give a clear view of the vertical adjustment mechanism.

Illus. 6-40. Because the Stanley #55 plane has a sliding section runner that can be vertically adjusted, it can be used to cut edge mouldings that cannot be cut with the other planes. The moulding being cut here is called a Grecian ogee. When you need to make several lengths of narrow moulding, start with a wide board and cut the moulding on both edges. Then rip the mouldings off with a saw and cut two more lengths of mouldings. You can continue like this until the board becomes too narrow to work with.

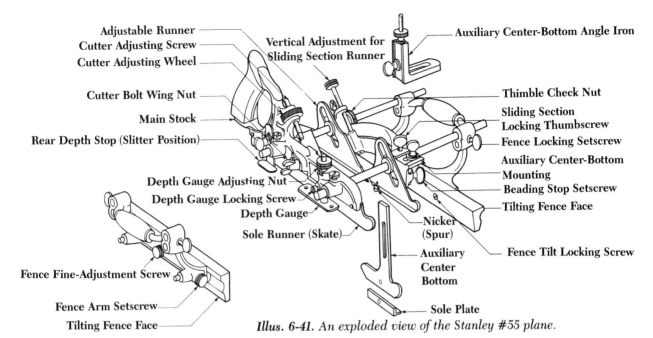

Adjustable Runner
Cutter Adjusting Screw
Cutter Adjusting Wheel
Vertical Adjustment for Sliding Section Runner
Auxiliary Center-Bottom Angle Iron
Cutter Bolt Wing Nut
Main Stock
Rear Depth Stop (Slitter Position)
Thimble Check Nut
Sliding Section Locking Thumbscrew
Fence Locking Setscrew
Auxiliary Center-Bottom Mounting
Beading Stop Setscrew
Tilting Fence Face
Depth Gauge Adjusting Nut
Depth Gauge Locking Screw
Depth Gauge
Sole Runner (Skate)
Nicker (Spur)
Fence Tilt Locking Screw
Fence Fine-Adjustment Screw
Auxiliary Center Bottom
Fence Arm Setscrew
Tilting Fence Face
Sole Plate

Illus. 6-41. An exploded view of the Stanley #55 plane.

It is used to provide additional support for the plane when the shape being worked doesn't have enough bearing surfaces for the main-stock runner or the sliding section runner. If the bearing surface that the auxiliary center bottom rides on is wider than ¼ inch, you can provide additional support by attaching the sole plate to the bottom of the auxiliary runner. The Stanley #55 plane has an additional fence that can be used to guide the work from both edges, and the faces of the fences can be set at an angle (Illus. 6-42).

Chamfering

Chamfering can be done with a standard bench plane held at a 45-degree angle, but you must rely on your eyes to get a uniform width and angle. (A

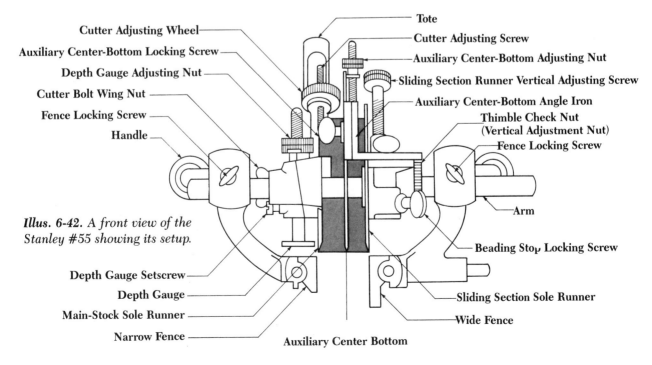

Cutter Adjusting Wheel
Auxiliary Center-Bottom Locking Screw
Depth Gauge Adjusting Nut
Cutter Bolt Wing Nut
Fence Locking Screw
Handle
Tote
Cutter Adjusting Screw
Auxiliary Center-Bottom Adjusting Nut
Sliding Section Runner Vertical Adjusting Screw
Auxiliary Center-Bottom Angle Iron
Thimble Check Nut (Vertical Adjustment Nut)
Fence Locking Screw
Arm
Beading Stop Locking Screw

Illus. 6-42. A front view of the Stanley #55 showing its setup.

Depth Gauge Setscrew
Depth Gauge
Main-Stock Sole Runner
Narrow Fence
Auxiliary Center Bottom
Sliding Section Sole Runner
Wide Fence

chamfer is a bevelled cut made on an edge.) If you will be making a number of chamfers, you can set up the #55 plane to accurately cut chamfers of uniform width and at the correct angle. If you use a hollow cutter instead of a straight cutter, you can make rounded corners using the same basic technique.

To set up the plane for chamfering, install a wide straight cutter. Install the auxiliary center bottom and the sliding section. Loosen the fence screws and adjust the fences to the correct angle; usually the angle will be 45 degrees, but you can make the chamfer at other angles if desired. Place the wide fence on the left side of the plane and the narrow fence on the right side of the plane.

Now, adjust the left fence and the sliding section so that when the plane is in position for the first stroke, the runner on the sliding section will touch the wood 1/32 inch to the right of the corner of the board. Set the auxiliary center bottom 1/8 inch away from the sliding section. The right fence acts as a depth stop. Adjust it so that it will touch the board when the chamfer is the desired width (Illus. 6-43).

It is a good idea to test the setup on a scrap board first and make any fine adjustments needed.

You can make a stopped chamfer by clamping a board to the work. Place the stop block so that the runners will hit it when the cutter is at the position you wish to stop the chamfer.

Cutting Mouldings

When the #55 plane was in production, there were a variety of moulding cutters available that would produce a complex moulding with a single setup. Some were included in the standard set of cutters, and others were optional cutters. If you can find a used #55 plane with a complete set of cutters, you will have the standard moulding cutters. The optional cutters are no longer being produced, and they are hard to find. All of these cutters are designed to cut a moulding on the edge of a board, but they can also be used on the face of the board and in combination with other cutters to make complex mouldings.

The moulding cutters come in six styles, with various sizes of each style (Illus. 6-44). The *quarter-hollow* cutter cuts an ovolo. The *quarter-round* cutter cuts a cove. The *reverse ogee* cutter makes a reverse ogee. The *Roman ogee* cutter cuts a Roman ogee. The *Grecian* ogee cutter cuts a Grecian ogee. The *quarter-round-with-bead* cutter cuts a cove and bead.

When cutting mouldings, it is important to use

Illus. 6-43. The Stanley #55 plane set up for chamfering.

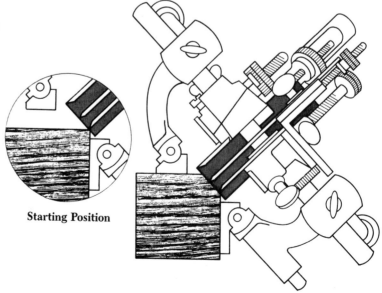

Starting Position

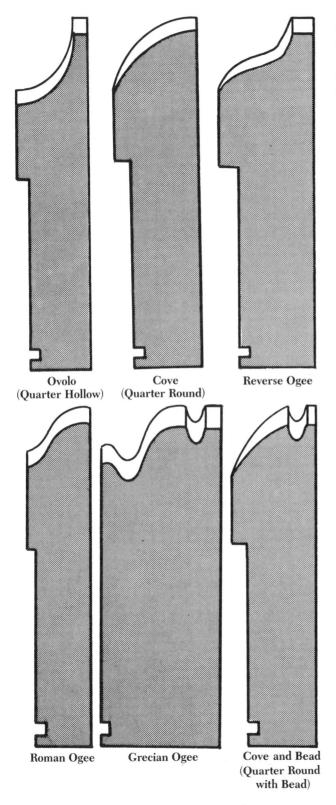

Ovolo
(Quarter Hollow)

Cove
(Quarter Round)

Reverse Ogee

Roman Ogee

Grecian Ogee

Cove and Bead
(Quarter Round
with Bead)

Illus. 6-44. There are six styles of moulding cutters for the #55 plane with range of sizes for each style.

straight-grained, knot-free stock to achieve a smooth, chip-free surface. It is also important to keep the plane from rocking and to keep the fence firmly against the edge. If the plane slips sideways, the moulding can be ruined. Because the plane is not sprung like the traditional wooden moulding plane, some mouldings are more difficult to make. Some simple mouldings like an ovolo or Roman ogee can be difficult to make, because the curvature of the cutter tends to force the plane away from the edge. Mouldings that incorporate a bead or quirk that can guide the sole runners are much easier to cut. The Grecian ogee and the cove and bead are two of the easiest to guide for this reason.

Edge mouldings can be cut in two ways. The plane can either be positioned with its sole runners on the edge of the board or on the face of the board. With symmetrical mouldings like the cove or ovolo, there is little difference in the final result. Other moulding cutters will have a different effect, depending on which way they are used.

When cutting ovolos, Roman ogees, or reverse ogees on the edge of a board, use both fences on the plane. This will keep the plane from wandering away from the edge. Using both fences can make the plane more difficult to push because of a slight binding effect. This problem is minimized if the stock is straight and uniform in thickness.

It is not possible to use the second fence when the moulding is being cut with the sole runners on the face of the board. In this case, leave a small uncut section between the moulding and the edge of the board (Illus. 6-45). This section of wood will guide the cutter and keep it from wandering off the edge. After the moulding has been cut, you can plane off the excess with a bench plane.

If you have trouble keeping the plane from tipping over as you cut a moulding on the face of the board, you can use the cam rest to steady the plane. To do this, the arms must extend from both sides of the plane. Slide the cam rest onto the right side of the front arm. The cam rest will act as an outrigger to steady the plane. Adjust the cam so that it holds the arms level. After each stroke, rotate the cam slightly to compensate for the downward progress of the plane.

Plane Away Extra after Striking Moulding.

Illus. 6-45. When cutting some mouldings like an ovolo or Roman ogee, the curvature of the cutter tends to force the plane away from the edge. In this case, leave a small uncut section between the moulding and the edge of the board. This section of wood will guide the cutter and keep it from wandering off the edge. After the moulding has been cut, you can plane off the excess with a bench plane.

Moulding cutters work best when used on edge grain, but it is often necessary to cut a moulded edge on end grain, such as in the case of a tabletop. When cutting a moulding on end grain, it is especially important that the cutter be as sharp as possible. Choose one of the simpler shapes. The small bead of the Grecian ogee or the cove and bead doesn't work on end grain, because it tends to get chipped off. Cut the end grain edges first. As the cutter passes the edge of the board, it will cause some splitting. Clamp a backup board to the work to control the splitting. A backup board is just a scrap of the same thickness that is clamped to the edge of the board. The splitting will occur on the backup board instead of the work.

In the directions below, I give the initial setup for each of the six types of moulding cutters. The initial setup is made with the cutter adjusted, so that the cutting edge is flush with the bottom of the main-stock runner. After making the initial setup, readjust the cutter to the desired cutting depth.

The vertical position of the sliding section runner must be adjusted for all of these mouldings. To make the adjustment, loosen the two thumbscrews on the sliding section, and then loosen the two thimble check nuts. Turn the adjusting screw to raise or lower the runner. The auxiliary center bottom is used for some of the moulding setups. This is a short runner that can be placed between

the two main runners. It is attached with an angle iron that fits into a groove machined in the top of the sliding section. You can adjust it horizontally by loosening the thumbscrew on the sliding section and sliding the angle iron back and forth. Its vertical position is adjusted with the adjusting nut, and it is locked in place with a thumbscrew on the angle iron.

The cutting edge must project equally past all of the runners. If the runners were not adjusted properly during the initial setup, make minor adjustments to get the plane to cut correctly. You may not notice a problem until you have worked a moulding down to the point where the other runner will contact the wood. At this point, it may seem as if the cutter adjustment has changed. This has occurred because there is a slight difference in the settings of the runners. If the cut seems too fine, raise the sliding section runner slightly. If the cut is too rank, lower the sliding section runner slightly.

Cutting Ovolos The ovolo is a very popular moulding. It consists of a convex quarter-round area set off by flat fillets. The cutter used to make the ovolo is called a quarter-hollow. The ovolo is often used on the stiles and rails of panel doors. Adjust the sliding section of the plane so that the runner will ride on the outside fillet, and set its vertical adjustment so that the bottom is flush with the flat tip of the cutter.

The size of the inside fillet is regulated with the depth gauge, and the size of the outside fillet is determined by the fence setting (Illus. 6-46).

Cutting Coves A cove is a concave cut on the edge of a board. The cutter used to make the cove is called a quarter-round. To set up for a cove, adjust the sliding section runner so that it will ride on the flat area near the outside edge.

The size of the cove can be altered by changing the depth gauge setting. The fence should be butted up against the edge of the cutter (Illus. 6-47).

Cutting Cove-and-Bead Moulding Cove-and-bead moulding is easier to cut than a standard

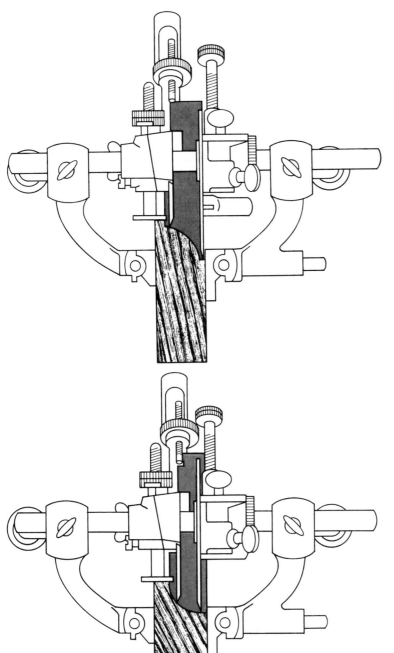

Illus. 6-46. The Stanley #55 plane set up to cut an ovolo.

Illus. 6-47. The Stanley #55 plane set up to cut a cove.

cove, because the bead helps to keep the plane on track. The curvature of a standard cove cutter tends to make the plane wander away from the edge. The bead projecting above the surface provides a guiding surface for the runner to ride against, counteracting the tendency of the plane to wander away from the edge.

To set up the plane, adjust the sliding section so that the outside edge of the runner will ride against the inside of the bead. Lower the runner until it is flush with the cutting edge at that point. The fence should be butted up against the edge of the cutter. The depth gauge is used to regulate the depth of the moulding (Illus. 6-48).

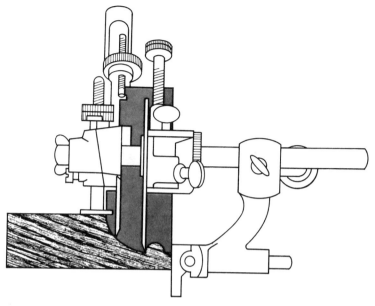

Illus. 6-48. *The Stanley #55 plane set up to cut a cove-and-bead moulding.*

Cutting Reverse Ogees To set up the plane for a reverse ogee, install the auxiliary center bottom (Illus. 6-49). Adjust the center bottom so that it rests at the transition point between the hollow and the round sections of the moulding. The sliding section runner should be flush with the left side of the cutter. Adjust the vertical position of the runner to be level with the flat at the tip of the cutter.

Set the depth gauge to control the depth of the moulding. Adjust the fence so that the flat of the cutter will produce a small quirk on the front edge. This will give the sliding section runner a flat area to run on, and the small section of wood left on the outside edge will prevent the plane from wandering off the edge. After the moulding is cut, you can remove the quirk with a block plane.

Cutting Roman Ogees When cutting a Roman ogee, there is a tendency for the plane to wander to the side. To prevent this, set the fence so that there is a small section of wood left between the cutter and the edge of the board. This extra wood can be trimmed off later with a bench plane.

Install the auxiliary center bottom and adjust it

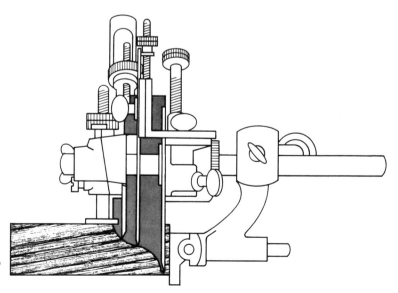

Illus. 6-49. *The Stanley #55 plane set up to cut a reverse ogee.*

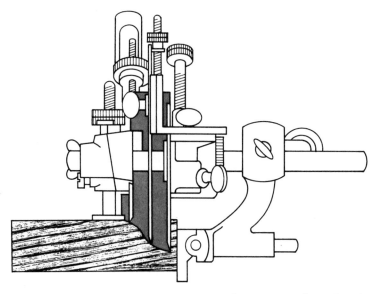

Illus. 6-50. The Stanley #55 plane set up to cut a Roman ogee.

to ride on the transition point near the center of the moulding. Adjust the sliding section runner so that its outside edge is flush with the outside edge of the cutter. Lower the vertical adjustment to bring the bottom of the runner flush with the tip of the cutter (Illus. 6-50).

On a Roman ogee, the transition from the top face of the board to the moulding can be a smooth, continuous curve. Adjust the depth gauge while you try the cut on scrap to achieve this smooth transition. If you prefer, you can set the depth gauge lower and form a fillet at the transition between the top and the moulded edge.

Cutting Grecian Ogees The Grecian ogee has a quirk and a bead. This gives both runners good bearing surfaces, so it is easy to guide the plane while making this moulding.

To set up the plane, adjust the sliding section runner so that it will ride against the inside edge of the bead. Set the vertical adjustment so that the bottom of the runner is flush with the cutting edge at this point.

The depth of the inside quirk is controlled by the depth gauge, and the width of the outside fillet is controlled by the fence position (Illus. 6-51).

Illus. 6-51. The Stanley #55 plane set up to cut a Grecian ogee.

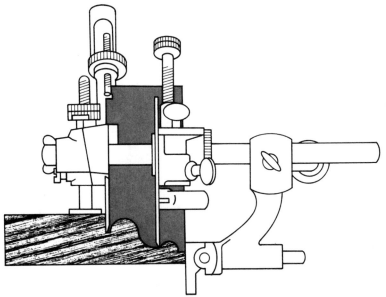

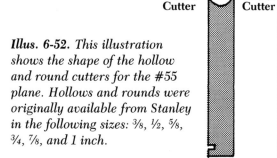

Illus. 6-52. This illustration shows the shape of the hollow and round cutters for the #55 plane. Hollows and rounds were originally available from Stanley in the following sizes: ⅜, ½, ⅝, ¾, ⅞, and 1 inch.

Cutting Hollows and Rounds Hollows and rounds are the basic shapes used to make virtually all other moulding profiles (Illus. 6-52). By combining them in different ways, you can reproduce a wide variety of mouldings. The hollow cutters make a convex shape. The setup for cutting with hollows is similar to the setup described for the beading cutters. Round cutters make a concave shape. They are similar to the fluting cutters described in the previous section, except they do not have the cutout section on their side to position the runner in the center.

To use rounds, you must adjust the vertical position of the sliding section runner. Adjust the cutter depth so that the cutting edge is flush with the bottom of the main-stock runner. Now, move the sliding section until its runner is centered on the cutter.

Next, lower the runner so that its bottom is flush with the cutting edge of the cutter. To adjust the vertical position of the runner, loosen the two thumbscrews that hold the sliding section in position on the arms and then loosen the two thimble check nuts. Now turn the adjusting screw to move the runner up or down. When the position of the runner is correct, tighten the thimble check nuts and then tighten the thumbscrews. Once the runner is adjusted, readjust the blade to make a fine cut.

When using hollows and rounds on the edge of the board, you can spring the plane to 45 degrees. This makes it easier to keep the plane from wandering than it is when using the moulding cutters described in the previous section. To spring the plane, set the faces of both fences to 45 degrees. One fence acts as a depth stop when this method is used.

A cove can be cut using the sprung plane method. Install a round cutter and set the fences to 45 degrees. Place one fence against the edge of the board and plane until the second fence touches the face of the board. The size of the cove is regulated by the position of the second fence, which acts as a depth stop.

To cut an ovolo using the sprung plane method, first cut the fillets with a plow cutter. Next, install a hollow cutter and spring the plane to 45 degrees. Use the hollow cutter to make the rounded section of the moulding.

You can make many other mouldings using hollows and rounds in combination with other cutters (Illus. 6–53—6–60). When much wood must be removed from one area, it is a good idea to rough-out the moulding using a plow cutter. The process of using hollows and rounds to make a complex moulding can be very time-consuming, but it can be invaluable if you need to duplicate a lost piece of moulding when you are restoring an antique.

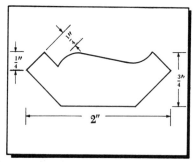

Illus. 6-53. This type of moulding is often used as a cornice on cabinets. (A cornice is a projecting moulding at the top of a piece of furniture.) The dimensions here are for a small cornice. You can make a larger moulding following these same proportions and using larger hollows and rounds.

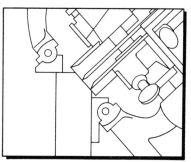

Illus. 6-54. Step 1: Start with a board that is wider than the finished moulding, to make clamping easier. Set up the plane for chamfering and make a 45-degree bevel on the rear edge of the board.

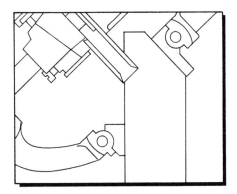

Illus. 6-55. *Step 2: Reset the wide fence to 90 degrees. Plow a V groove on the face of the board, using a ¼-inch-wide plow cutter. The wide fence rides against the chamfered edge. Use the narrow fence set to 45 degrees as a depth stop.*

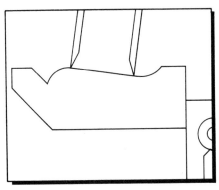

Illus. 6-58. *Step 5: Rip the moulding to width with a saw. Then set the fence to about 10 degrees and use a plow cutter to make the transition between the hollow and the round.*

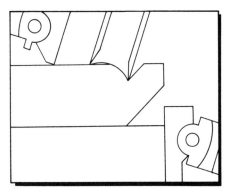

Illus. 6-56. *Step 3: Use a ½-inch-wide hollow cutter to make the next cut. Set the long fence to 20 degrees. Clamp a guide board to the back of the moulding for the fence to ride against. The narrow fence set to 90 degrees acts as a depth stop.*

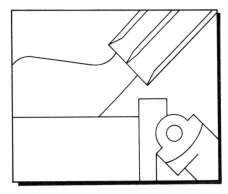

Illus. 6-59. *Step 6: Chamfer the other rear edge to 45 degrees, and then chamfer the front edges.*

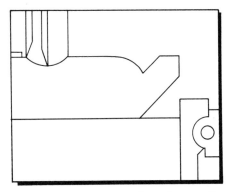

Illus. 6-57. *Step 4: Use a ½-inch-wide round cutter for this cut. Set the wide fence to 90 degrees. The narrow fence is not used. Control the depth with the adjustable depth gauge.*

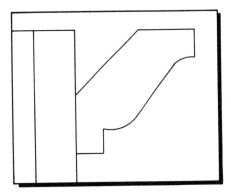

Illus. 6-60. *Step 7: Install the moulding on the cabinet. This type of moulding is installed so that it projects at a 45-degree angle. You can cut a triangular block to place behind the moulding, if you want.*

Chapter 7

SCRAPERS

When the wood grain is highly figured, it is difficult to plane it to a smooth surface, because its grain direction changes so frequently. In this case, a scraper can be used for the final finishing. The scraper leaves a smooth finish even on wild-grained woods. Scrapers work best on hardwoods. They aren't as effective on softwoods, but they are especially useful for smoothing wood around knots.

Scrapers have been used for a very long time, probably longer than planes. Before the widespread use of sandpaper, scrapers were almost universally used as the final step in surface preparation before applying a finish. The surface produced by a sharp scraper can be superior to that produced by even the finest sandpaper, so if you are serious about getting the smoothest possible surface, use a scraper (Illus. 7-1).

Scrapers use a different type of blade than a plane. The blade is held almost vertically, and the cutting is accomplished with a small burr on the edge of the blade (Illus. 7-2). Forming this burr involves a different sharpening procedure than that for a plane iron, but it is not hard to master.

The simplest type of scraper is the *hand scraper*. It is simply a steel blade that is held in your hands (Illus. 7-3). The hand scraper is very good for getting into tight places and smoothing around knots, but it is tiring to use a hand scraper to smooth a large surface.

The *cabinet scraper* has a cast-iron body that holds a scraper blade. This makes it easier to use on large surfaces. The flat sole of the cabinet scraper also helps to keep the cut uniform (Illus. 7-4).

Using a Hand Scraper

A hand scraper is simply a flat piece of tool steel that has a sharp burr on its edge. The edges are square with the face of the scraper. The simplest type has a rectangular shape. There are also scrapers that are shaped to fit various curved work surfaces (Illus. 7-5).

To use a hand scraper, grasp its edges with both hands and place your thumbs in the middle of the blade. The blade must have a slight bow to cut properly. Bow the blade by pressing in the middle with your thumbs. Hold the blade so that it is almost vertical, but with its top front edge tilted slightly away from you so that the angle is between 75 and 85 degrees. Make the cut by pushing the scraper away from your body. Always move the scraper parallel to the grain of the wood. Adjust the angle of the blade until you get the most efficient cut (Illus. 7-6 and 7-7). When cutting properly, the scraper will produce fine shavings. If it is producing dust, either you are holding it wrong or the blade is dull.

The hand scraper can get into corners and tight areas better than a cabinet scraper. It can also be very useful for smoothing wood around knots. You can vary the angle that you hold the blade at until you get the best cutting action over the knot.

As you use a hand scraper, you will note that your thumbs have quickly become tired from holding the bow in the blade, and that after a while, the blade has become hot enough to be uncomfortable to hold. This will not happen with a cabinet scraper, because it has a screw to bow the blade.

Illus. 7-1. The surface produced by a sharp scraper can be superior to that produced by even the finest sandpaper, so if you are serious about getting the smoothest possible surface, use a scraper.

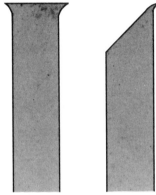

Illus. 7-2. Scrapers use a different type of blade than a plane. The cutting is accomplished with a small burr on the edge of the blade.

Hand Scraper   Cabinet Scraper

Illus. 7-3. The simplest type of scraper is the hand scraper. It is simply a steel blade that is held in your hands.

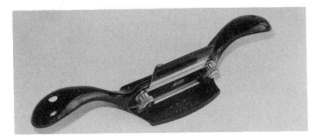

Illus. 7-4. The cabinet scraper has a cast-iron body that holds a scraper blade. This makes it easier to use on large surfaces. The flat sole of the cabinet scraper also helps to keep the cut uniform.

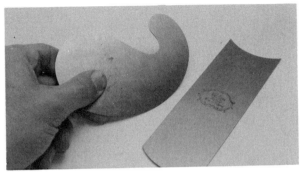

Illus. 7-5. Scrapers with curved edges can be useful for scraping mouldings and other curved sections of a project. The scraper on the left is called a gooseneck scraper; the one on the right is called a convex/concave scraper.

Illus. 7-6. To use a hand scraper, grasp its edges with both hands and place your thumbs in the middle of the blade. The blade must have a slight bow to cut properly. Bow the blade by pressing in the middle with your thumbs. Hold the blade so that it is almost vertical, but with its top front edge tilted a little away from you so that the angle is between 75 degrees and 85 degrees.

Illus. 7-7. To use a gooseneck scraper, first find the section of the blade that matches the contour of the work. If you are using the long edge of the blade, you can use it just like the standard scraper; use both hands and bow it slightly. When you are using the gooseneck section, as shown here, it may not be possible to get both hands comfortably on the blade. In this case, it is not necessary to bow the scraper; just hold it at a 75-to-85-degree angle.

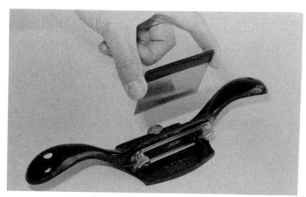

Illus. 7-8. The cabinet scraper has a cast-iron body. The scraper blade is clamped in place with two thumbscrews, and a third thumbscrew is used to bow the blade. The blade is similar to a hand scraper blade, but its edge is ground to a 45-degree bevel. The blade projects through a mouth in the sole of the cast-iron body.

Using a Cabinet Scraper

The cabinet scraper has a cast-iron body. The scraper blade is clamped in place with two thumbscrews, and a third thumbscrew is used to bow the blade (Illus. 7-8). The blade is similar to a hand scraper blade, but the edge is ground to a 45-degree bevel. The blade projects through a mouth in the sole of the cast-iron body.

To set up the scraper, adjust the height of the blade by loosening all three thumbscrews. Set the scraper sole down on a flat board and let the edge of the blade rest on the surface of the board. Now, tighten the clamp screws. This gives you the initial setting for the blade. The depth of cut is regulated by tightening the third thumbscrew to bow the blade. The more bow there is in the blade, the deeper the cut will be.

The cabinet scraper is normally pushed away from your body, but it can also be pulled towards you when that would be more convenient for a particular job. The blade is bowed out on the front. Make sure that you are holding the scraper so that the blade is oriented with the bow facing forward. Make a test cut on some scrap to make the first adjustments. Turn in the thumbscrew until the scraper starts cutting, and then adjust the blade for the best cut.

To scrape the surface of a board, start at one edge and let the scraper blade overhang the edge about halfway. Make one long continual stroke from one end to the other. Then move the scraper over and make another stroke, overlapping the first one about halfway. Continue like this until you have scraped the entire surface. If there is a particularly difficult area that can't be smoothed with the cabinet scraper, go over that section with a hand scraper and adjust the angle until you get a smooth cut.

Sharpening Scrapers

A sharp scraper will cut shavings like a plane, only thinner and shorter. If it just makes dust, it is dull and should be resharpened. The processes for sharpening the hand scraper and the cabinet scraper blade are similar. The one difference is that the edge of a hand scraper blade is ground to 90 degrees, and the edge of a cabinet scraper blade is ground to 45 degrees.

The first step is to remove the old burr. This can be done with a fine file or a whetstone. To file the edge, place the blade between two pieces of wood in a vise. Use a smooth mill file to first file the face and then the edge of the blade to remove the old burr. The file should be held square and not allowed to rock during this step (Illus. 7-9). When filing the cabinet scraper blade, follow the original angle of 45 degrees (Illus. 7-10).

Now, switch to a whetstone and hone the edge of the blade (Illus. 7-11). The hand scraper is held in a vertical position, and the cabinet scraper is held at a 45-degree angle. After honing the edge, back off the blade on the stone by placing the back of the blade flat on the stone and rubbing it back and forth several times (Illus. 7-12). The procedure up to this point has been similar to that for sharpening a plane iron. The next step is unique to scrapers; it is called *burnishing*.

The burnishing process forms a sharp burr on the cutting edge. To do this, you need a rod of hardened steel. You can use a special tool called a

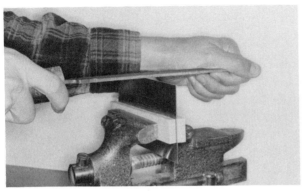

Illus. 7-9. Filing is necessary to remove nicks from the cutting edge of a scraper. If the edge is in good condition, you can skip this step and proceed directly to the whetstone. To file the edge of a hand scraper blade, place the blade between two pieces of wood in a vise. Use a smooth mill file to first file the face and then the edge of the blade, to remove the old burr. The file should be held square and not allowed to rock during this step.

Illus. 7-12. After honing the edge, back off the blade on the stone by placing the back of the blade flat on the stone and rubbing it back and forth several times.

Illus. 7-10. When filing the cabinet scraper blade, follow the original angle of 45 degrees.

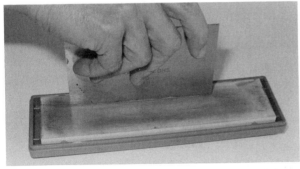

Illus. 7-11. Use a whetstone to hone the edge of the blade. The hand scraper is held in a vertical position, and the cabinet scraper is held at a 45-degree angle.

burnisher that looks like an oval file with no teeth, or you can use an awl. There is also a special tool called a wheel burnisher that does a very good job.

Hold the blade on the edge of the bench with its edge overhanging the edge of the bench, or place it edge-up in a vise with padded jaws. Wipe a drop of oil onto the burnisher. Hold the burnisher flat against the face and pull it across the edge about four times. Next, place the burnisher against the edge and hold it flat against the edge. For a hand scraper, this will be 90 degrees (Illus. 7-13). For a cabinet scraper, hold the burnisher at a 45-degree angle (Illus. 7-14). Pull the burnisher across the edge about four times, and then change the angle of the burnisher slightly to put the proper hook angle on the burr. Keep making strokes and increasing the angle until a good burr is formed.

The hook angle of the burr can be varied to suit the work. (The hook angle is the angle of the burr's cutting edge as it relates to the centerline of the blade.) For very fine work like marquetry or veneer, use a zero-degree hook angle. To get a zero-degree hook angle on a hand scraper, do all of the burnishing with the burnisher held at 90 degrees. To get a zero-degree hook angle on a cabinet scraper, keep the burnisher flat against the 45-degree bevel of the blade.

For most uses, a hook angle around 5 degrees is good. To burnish a 5-degree hook angle, gradually lift the handle of the burnisher after each stroke until the angle of the burnisher is 5 degrees

Illus. 7-13. *To begin burnishing, hold the blade on the edge of the bench with the edge overhanging the edge, or place it edge-up in a vise with padded jaws, as shown here. Wipe a drop of oil onto the burnisher. The burnisher being used in this case is an oval type made specifically for burnishing scrapers. Hold the burnisher flat against the face of the blade and pull it across the edge about four times. Next, place the burnisher against the edge of the blade and hold it flat. For a hand scraper, this will be at 90 degrees. Pull the burnisher across the edge about four times, keeping the burnisher at a 90-degree angle. Now, change the angle of the burnisher slightly. Keep taking strokes and increasing the angle until a good burr is formed.*

greater than it was when you started. For a hand scraper, the burnisher will be at a 95-degree angle. For a cabinet scraper, the burnisher angle will be 50 degrees.

When you want to remove more wood with each stroke of the scraper, use a hook angle of between 5 and 10 degrees. For heavy work, use a hook angle of 10 to 15 degrees. A 15-degree hook angle is good when you are using the scraper to remove glue drips, old paint, or varnish.

The process is considerably simpler with a *wheel burnisher*. This is a hardened steel wheel that is mounted in a wooden stock. The wheel burnisher will produce the correct burr if you simply place the fence of the stock against the face of the blade and pull the burnisher across the edge.

The *variable burnisher* is similar to a wheel burnisher, but it uses a carbide rod mounted in a

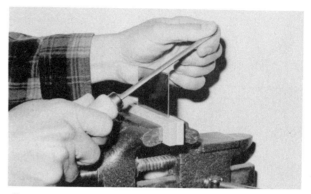

Illus. 7-14. *To burnish a cabinet scraper, use the same procedure, but start with the burnisher held at a 45-degree angle.*

wooden stock. A knob on the front allows you to accurately adjust the hook angle.

To use either a wheel burnisher or a variable burnisher, clamp the scraper in a vise padded with wood blocks. Apply a drop of oil to the edge, and then place the groove in the burnisher stock over the scraper blade. Push down hard on the burnisher and pull it across the scraper blade (Illus. 7-15). Don't push the burnisher, because at the end of the stroke you may hit the palm of your hand on the scraper blade and injure your hand.

The first two or three passes over the blade should be made with the variable burnisher set to zero degrees. After that, you can set the dial to the hook angle you want and make two or three more passes over the blade.

Illus. 7-15. *This burnisher uses a carbide rod to burnish the edge. The hook angle can be varied by adjusting the dial on the front of the burnisher. Be sure to pull the burnisher; don't push it or your palm may hit the scraper blade.*

Chapter 8

A PLANING PROJECT

In this chapter, I demonstrate how the different planes and techniques described in the previous chapters can be used together in a single project, in this case a Shaker jelly cupboard (Illus. 8-1). I have included a plan and bill of materials for the project, so if you would like to get some experience using planes, you can build one of these cupboards (Illus. 8-2). Even if you don't build this project, this chapter will give you a better idea of

Illus. 8-1. The various techniques described in this book can be used together to make a project such as this Shaker jelly cupboard.

how the various planing techniques are used in the construction of a cabinet.

I will be concentrating on the planing operations of the project. Of course, other tools and techniques are necessary to build this type of project. If you need more detail about the other joinery operations, consult my books *Wood Joiner's Handbook* or *Joinery Basics*.

Surfacing the Stock

I will be starting with rough pine boards that are 1 inch thick. You could use boards that have been surfaced at the mill, but I want to demonstrate the full range of the planing process using hand planes.

Since antiques were built using wood that was surfaced by hand, the thickness of the wood usually varied, in contrast to the standard ¾-inch-thick lumber used today. In many cases, the wood used was ⅞ inch thick. Some pieces may have boards of several different thicknesses. This project uses ¾-, ⅝-, ⅞-, and ¹⁵⁄₁₆-inch-thick wood. If you want to make a project look like it is a real antique, surfacing the boards with hand planes allows you to choose the appropriate thickness and eliminate any traces of modern tool marks.

Start by checking the wood for warping, winding, and variations in thickness. (Warping is a bow, cup, or twist in a board. Winding is a twist in a board.) Cut the wood to rough length and cut out troublesome sections such as large knots or badly warped areas. The sides, shelves, and top are wider than most commonly available lumber, so you may have to glue up two or more boards to get the correct width. After cutting them to rough length, lay the boards side by side and decide how to glue them together. To minimize cupping problems, alternate the direction of the rings, that is, arrange the boards so that the curvature of the tree rings faces up on one board and down on the next. It will be simpler to plane the glued-up panels if the grain is running in the same direction on all of the boards in the panel.

It is fairly easy to tell the grain direction on rough lumber. Look closely at the rough fibres on the surface; the broken ends of the fibres point in the direction you should push the plane. When you glue up the boards, place them so that the rough fibres are all pointing in the same direction. Mark the boards so that you can tell which boards go together.

Before you can glue up the boards, you will need to joint the mating edges, that is, prepare the board for joining by planing its edges (Illus. 8-4). Usually, I like to joint the edges of a board after the faces are planed, but in this case, you must joint the edges while the face is still rough. To avoid a splinter, place your hand on top of the plane instead of wrapping your fingers around the fore end of the plane, as you do when jointing surfaced lumber.

When you have jointed the edges, glue up the panels. I use a few dowels on the edges to help

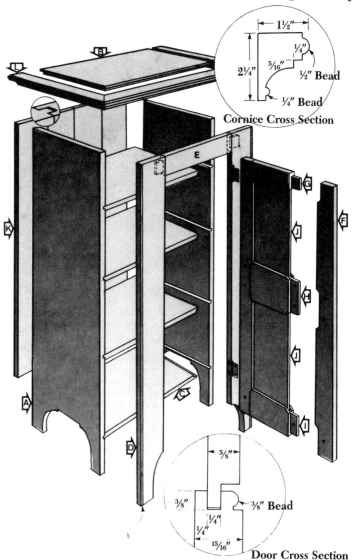

Illus. 8-2. *An exploded view of the Shaker jelly cupboard.*

TABLE 8-1
Shaker Jelly Cupboard
Bill of Materials

Part	Quantity	Description	Size
A	2	sides	$\frac{7}{8} \times 14\frac{1}{16} \times 51\frac{1}{4}''$
B	1	top	$\frac{7}{8} \times 15 \times 20''$
C	4	shelves	$\frac{3}{4} \times 13\frac{5}{16} \times 19''$
D	2	face-frame stiles	$\frac{15}{16} \times 4 \times 51\frac{1}{4}''$
E	1	face-frame rail	$\frac{15}{16} \times 3 \times 14\frac{1}{2}''$ (includes $1\frac{1}{4}''$ tenons)
F	2	door stiles	$\frac{15}{16} \times 2\frac{1}{2} \times 44\frac{3}{4}''$ (includes $1''$ horns)
G	1	door top rail	$\frac{15}{16} \times 3 \times 9\frac{1}{2}''$ (includes $1\frac{1}{4}''$ tenons)
H	1	door center rail	$\frac{15}{16} \times 5 \times 9\frac{1}{2}''$ (includes $1\frac{1}{4}''$ tenons)
I	1	door bottom rail	$\frac{15}{16} \times 4 \times 9\frac{1}{2}''$ (includes $1\frac{1}{4}''$ tenons)
J	2	door panels	$\frac{5}{8} \times 7\frac{1}{2} \times 16\frac{1}{8}''$
K	4	back tongue-and-groove boards	$\frac{3}{4} \times 5\frac{5}{16} \times 45\frac{3}{4}''$ (includes $\frac{1}{4}''$ tongue)
L	1	cornice moulding	$1\frac{1}{2} \times 2\frac{1}{4} \times 72''$ (long enough for 3 pieces)

Bill of materials for the Shaker jelly cupboard. All the parts are made of pine. All the dimensions are in inches. See Illus. 8-2, which shows the different parts of the cupboard.

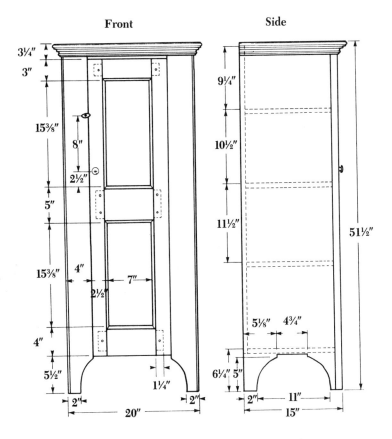

***Illus. 8-3.** Plans for the Shaker jelly cupboard.*

Illus. 8-4. The sides, shelves, and top are wider than most commonly available lumber, so you may need to glue up two or more boards to get the correct width. Before you can glue up the boards, you will have to joint the mating edges. To avoid a splinter in your fingers, place your hand on top of the plane.

Illus. 8-5. After the glue is dry, remove the clamps and begin surfacing the lumber. Start with a jack plane. Make a rank cut, to remove the saw marks. Plane across the face at about a 45-degree angle.

Illus. 8-6. Once the saw marks are gone, switch to the trying plane. At first, plane across the face of the board at about a 45-degree angle, such as you did with the jack plane. This will remove any cupping in the board.

Illus. 8-7. When the plane is cutting evenly across the face of the board, reposition the plane so that it is parallel to the board's edges, and plane in long, straight strokes along the full length of the board. Overlap each stroke slightly until you have planed across the entire face.

keep the boards in alignment during the clamping. The glue joint will be strong enough without dowels, so you don't have to use them. They are most useful when you are trying to get the maximum thickness possible out of the board. When the boards are of sufficient thickness, you can simply plane away any slight misalignment.

After the glue is dry, remove the clamps and begin surfacing the lumber. The wood I am using is fairly uniform in thickness and flat, so I will begin planing with the jack plane. If there were high spots or misaligned joints that needed special attention, a scrub plane could be used to work them down.

Now, begin to plane the first face with a jack plane. Make a rank cut, to remove the saw marks. Plane across the face at about a 45-degree angle (Illus. 8-5). You can actually begin with the trying plane set rank to remove the saw marks, but there is always some sand and dirt trapped in the rough fibres of the surface. I like to remove the rough surface with a jack plane and save the keen edge of my trying plane for the finer work.

Once you have eliminated the saw marks, switch to the trying plane. At first, plane across the face with about a 45-degree angle, such as you did with the jack plane (Illus. 8-6). This will remove any cupping in the board.

When the plane is cutting evenly across the face of the board, reposition the plane so that it is parallel to the edges, and plane in long, straight strokes along the full length of the board (Illus. 8-7). Overlap each stroke slightly until you have planed across the entire face.

As you plane, observe where the plane is cutting and where it is not. At first, the plane will only cut across the high spots. As you work down the high spots, the plane will make longer and longer cuts until it is cutting the full length of the board. Stop planing as soon as you create a flat surface. Mark this face for future reference.

Some of the boards in this project are ⅞ inch thick at their finished sizes. If you are starting with 1-inch-thick lumber, this only leaves 1/16 inch of wood that can be removed on each side. To do this, you must start with flat boards. If you must remove a lot of cupping or other defects, you will have to remove more wood. You can either settle for a ¾-inch-thick board or start with a thicker piece of rough lumber.

The face frame and door frame are ¹⁵⁄₁₆ inch thick. You can't get a thickness of ¹⁵⁄₁₆ inch from a board that starts out 1 inch thick. If you sort through a pile of rough boards, you will usually find a few that are thicker than the rest; if the board is about 1⅛ inches thick and fairly flat, you can get the ¹⁵⁄₁₆-inch-thick parts from it. If you can't find an appropriate piece of rough lumber, either make these parts ⅞ inch thick or buy lumber that is 1½ inches thick and plane it down to ¹⁵⁄₁₆ inch.

Next, set the marking gauge for the required thickness and gauge a line on all four edges of the board. If the edges are too rough to mark, plane them with the jack plane first. At this point, you aren't trying to joint the edge; just make it smooth enough for the gauge line to show.

Now, place the board on the bench rough-side-up and repeat the planing procedure. Use the jack plane to remove the saw marks and get close to the gauged line. Then switch to the trying plane and flatten the surface and bring the thickness to the gauged line.

When there is a lot of wood to be removed, as is the case for the ⅝-inch-thick door panels, you may want to start with the scrub plane. Set the iron rank and plane diagonally across the face. After a while, reverse the board and plane diagonally from the other direction. When you start to get close to the gauged line, switch to the jack plane. Use the jack plane to smooth out the washboard left by the scrub plane and bring the thickness of the board closer to the gauged line. (A washboard is a wavy pattern left by the cambered iron of the scrub plane.) Finally, switch to the trying plane to flatten the surface. Stop planing when you reach the gauged line.

Jointing the Edges

Next, use a jointer or trying plane to joint one edge of the board (Illus. 8-8). (Jointing is the process of truing the edges so that they are straight and square with the face.) Pick the straightest edge and place the board in the vise with that

Illus. 8-8. Use a jointer plane or a trying plane to joint one edge of the board. Pick the straightest edge and place the board in the vise with that edge up. Support the end of long boards with a peg on the bench front.

edge up. Support the end of long boards with a peg on the bench front. Hold the plane so that its sole is square with the face of the board. Plane in one long, continuous stroke from one end to the other. Keep working down the edge until the plane is cutting continuously from end to end. Check the edge with a square to make sure that it is 90 degrees to the face. If necessary, make corrections by planing down the high side of the edge.

Now, using the jointed edge for a reference, lay out the width of the boards, Rip the boards to width with a table saw or a hand ripsaw. Leave the boards about ¹⁄₁₆ inch wider than their final widths. After ripping them to width, use the jointer plane to smooth their edges and bring the boards to their final width.

Smoothing the Stock

The final step in surfacing the stock is smoothing it with a smooth plane. Where the thickness of the board is crucial to a tight-fitting joint, do all of the planing before cutting the joints. On surfaces that aren't critical for ensuring a tight-fitting joint, it is better to wait until just before assembly to use the smooth plane. This way, all of the dings and smudges that get on the surface while you are working will be removed.

The critical faces of this project are the tops of the shelves and the rear of the panels. Adjust the smooth plane for a very fine cut. Hold the plane skewed about 10 degrees and make straight strokes the length of the boards. Overlap each stroke slightly and only remove enough wood to create a smooth surface. At this stage, you should be producing shavings that are as thin as onionskin.

Making Rabbets and Dadoes

The top is rabbeted to fit over the sides. The shelves and bottom fit into dadoes. Before cutting the dadoes, place the two sides of the cupboard (part A) on the bench with their inside faces up and their front edges butted together. Use bar clamps to hold the boards tightly together. Clamping them together like this ensures that the joints will line up and you can cut the dadoes in both boards at the same time.

Once you have the boards clamped together, check to make sure that their ends are square and that both boards are the same length. If they are out of square or slightly different in size, use a sharp knife and a straightedge to score a line. Then plane the ends to the line using a smooth plane. Work in from both edges to the middle to avoid splitting the edges. Now, lay out the positions of the dadoes as shown in Illus. 8-9.

Illus. 8-9. To cut the dadoes on the sides of the cup-board, place the two sides with their inside faces facing up on the bench with their front edges butted together. Use bar clamps to hold the boards tightly together. Use a guide board about 1½ inches wide and ¼ inch thick. Line up the edge of the guide board with the layout line for the first dado and tack it in place with short nails. Set up the plow combination plane to make a ½-inch-wide dado.

To make the dadoes, set up the plow combination plane to make a cross-grain cut by installing the sliding section and lowering the nickers. Bare-faced tongue-and-groove joints will be used, so the dado is less than the actual thickness of the boards. Install the ½-inch cutter in the plane. Cut a guide board about 1½ inches wide and ¼ inch thick. Line up the edge of the guide board with the layout line for the first dado and tack it in place with short nails. Put a nail near each edge and one near the middle. In this instance, it is not necessary to use a backup board, because the rear edge of the board will be rabbeted later, so any splintering will be planed away as the rabbet is made.

The depth stop will ride on the guide board, so allow for the additional ¼ inch when you set it. The dado should be ⅜ inch deep. Place the plane at the toe end of the cut and pull it rearwards to scribe the shoulders with the nickers. Now, start at the heel end and plane across the boards until you reach the depth stop. Move the guide board to the next location and repeat until all of the dadoes are cut (Illus. 8-9).

Next, cut the rabbets. Use a fillister to cut the rabbet between the top and the sides. Set the fence for ⅞ inch. Set the depth stop for 7/16 inch. This is a cross-grain rabbet, so turn down the nicker and use a backup board.

Place the fillister at the toe end of the board and align the fence with the end of the board. Pull the plane rearwards across the board to scribe a line with the nicker. Now, start at the heel end of the board and plane across the boards repeatedly until the depth stop hits the face (Illus. 8-10).

Next, make the rabbet along the rear edge of the two sides and the rear of the top. Use the fillister to make the rabbet. Since this is a cut with the grain, the nicker is not used (Illus. 8-11). The rabbet cut in the top goes from end to end, but the rabbet on the sides is stopped at the bottom dado. You can make the stopped rabbet by placing the fillister iron in the bullnose position. Since the rabbet stops at a dado, you don't have to chisel out the end of the rabbet. However, the ½-inch width of the dado doesn't give you much room to stop the plane, so it is easy to overshoot the dado. To prevent this, clamp a piece of scrap to the side

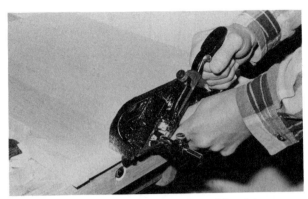

Illus. 8-10. Use a fillister to cut the rabbet between the top and the sides. Set the fence for 7/8 inch. Set the depth stop to 7/16 inch. This is a cross-grain rabbet, so turn down the nicker and use a backup board.

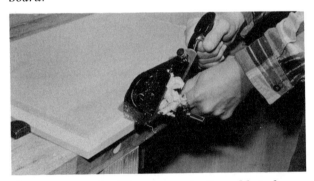

Illus. 8-11. Use the fillister to make the rabbet along the rear edge of the top, as shown here, and the rear edge of the two sides. Since this is a cut with the grain, the nicker is not used.

Illus. 8-12. The rabbet in the sides is stopped at the bottom dado. You can make the stopped rabbet by placing the fillister iron in the bullnose position. Since the rabbet stops at a dado, you don't have to chisel out the end of the rabbet. To prevent over-shooting the dado, clamp a piece of scrap to the side even with the far shoulder of the dado.

even with the far shoulder of the dado (Illus. 8-12).

When making the stopped rabbets, you must plane the right side in a different direction from the left side. The left side can be planed with the fillister set up as usual. To plane the right side, remove the fence and unscrew the fence arm. Reinstall the fence arm on the opposite side of the plane and reinstall the fence. You will now be able to plane into the stopped end of the right-side rabbet, but the depth gauge will not work with the plane set up this way. This isn't a great problem, because the rabbet is planed to the same depth as the dadoes. Just keep planing until the rabbet is flush with the bottoms of the dadoes. Next, reset the fence on the fillister to 15/16 inch and make the rabbet on the front edge of the top.

To complete the barefaced tongue-and-groove joint (pages 59 and 60), you must plane a rabbet on the ends of the shelves. Use the fillister to make the rabbets. Set the fence for 3/8 inch. Set the depth stop for the difference between the width of the dado and the thickness of the boards. The dado in this case is 1/2 inch. the shelf boards are 3/4 inch thick, so the depth stop should be set to 1/4 inch. Since hand-planed boards can vary slightly in thickness, it is a good idea to gauge a line on the end of the boards from the face opposite the rabbet with the gauge set to 1/2 inch. As you plane the rabbet, watch the line and stop when you reach it, even if you haven't reached the depth stop.

Clamp a backup board to the far edge of the shelf to prevent splintering and cut the rabbet with the fillister. Repeat the procedure on the other end and on all of the other shelves (Illus. 8-13). If you would like a rounded edge on the shelves, use a radius plane to round over the front edge after you have completed the rabbet cuts (Illus. 8-14).

The Face Frame

The face frame consists of the two stiles (Part D in Illus. 8-1) and the top rail (Part E in Illus. 8-2). The top rail is attached to the stiles with mortise-and-tenon joints. Begin by chopping the mortises in the stiles with a mortise chisel. The mortise

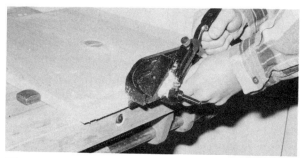

Illus. 8-13. *To complete the barefaced tongue-and-groove joint, you must plane a rabbet on the end of the shelves. Use the fillister to make the rabbets. Set the fence for ⅜ inch. Set the depth stop for ¼ inch.*

Illus. 8-14. *If you would like a rounded edge on the shelves, use a radius plane to round over the front edge after you have completed the rabbet cuts.*

Illus. 8-15. *Chop the mortises in the stiles with a mortise chisel.*

Illus. 8-16. *Use the fillister to make the tenons.*

Illus. 8-17. *Trim the tenons with a backsaw so that they fit the mortise.*

Illus. 8-18. *If it is necessary to clean up the tenon shoulders, make a very fine cut with a shoulder plane.*

Illus. 8-19. *Use the universal combination plane to cut the ⅜-inch bead along the outside edge of the front stiles.*

should be ⅜ inch wide, 2 inches long, and 1¼ inches deep (Illus. 8-15).

Next, lay out the tenons with a marking gauge. Score along the shoulder mark with a sharp knife to make sure that you get a clean cut. Now, set up the fillister to cut the tenons. Turn down the nicker because this is a cross-grain cut. Set the fence for 1¼ inches. Clamp the rail to the bench with a backup board and plane the first cheek of the tenon. Keep an eye on the layout lines and stop when you reach them. Now, turn over the board and repeat the process for the other cheek (Illus. 8-16). Then cut the tenon on the other end of the rail.

Since this tenon doesn't run the full width of the rail, trim it with a backsaw so that it fits the mortise (Illus. 8-17). If it is necessary to clean up the shoulders, make a very fine cut with a shoulder plane (Illus. 8-18).

There is a ⅜-inch bead along the outside edge of the front stiles. Set up a universal combination plane to cut the bead. Install a ⅜-inch bead cutter and set the fence so that the outside quirk of the bead is entirely covered by the fence. Make a test cut on a piece of scrap to make sure that the bead is fully rounded on its edge but that there is no trace of the outside quirk. Work down the bead on both stiles. The bead should be about ¹⁄₁₆ inch lower than the face of the stile (Illus. 8-19).

Assembling the Carcass

Now is a good time to assemble the carcass. Once the carcass is assembled, you can measure the door opening and the back and make any adjustments necessary when you build the door and make the boards for the back. Start by applying glue to the tongues on the shelves and the dadoes on one of the sides. Insert the shelves into the dadoes. Note that the rabbet is on the top face of the bottom shelf. The rabbet on the remaining shelves is on the underside face of the shelves.

Next, apply glue to the other side and place the side on top of the shelves. A helper is very useful at this stage of assembly, because you must line up all of the shelves with the dadoes. When the side is in place, clamp the carcass together with bar clamps.

Check the carcass for square by measuring the diagonals from the top corner of one side to the bottom corner of the other. The two measurements should be the same. If they are not, realign the carcass until the diagonals are equal. Temporarily tack a board diagonally across the back to hold the carcass square.

Secure the shelves to the sides with finish nails. If you nail from the inside, there will be no visible nail holes on the outside of the cabinet. This is called toenailing. Drive the nails diagonally into the underside of the shelf right at the point where the shelf touches the side. Make the angle steep enough so that the point of the nail will not break-out on the face of the side. When the nail head gets too close to the shelf for you to use the hammer alone, use a nail set to drive the nails. Three or four nails per joint is sufficient.

After the joints have been secured with nails, remove the clamps and install the top. Apply glue to the rabbets on the ends of the top and attach the top to the carcass (Illus. 8-20). Drive nails through the sides into the top. These nails will be concealed when the cornice moulding is applied.

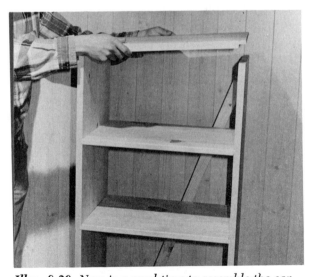

Illus. 8-20. Now is a good time to assemble the carcass. Once the carcass is assembled, you can measure the door opening and the back and make any adjustments necessary when you build the door and make the boards for the back.

Now, attach the face frame to the carcass. Apply glue to the mortise-and-tenon joints and insert the rail tenons into the mortises in the stiles. Apply glue to the front edge of the sides and the front rabbet on the top, and then put the face frame in place. Clamp the face frame in position and then secure it with finish nails spaced about 8 inches apart. Drive the nails into the quirk of the bead on the front stiles. This is a very effective way to conceal the nails. Use a nail set to drive the head into the quirk and set it below the bottom of the quirk. Apply a dab of wood putty to cover the nail head. After the putty is dry, wrap a piece of sandpaper around a thin piece of wood or cardboard that will fit into the quirk. You will use this to sand the putty smooth and flush with the bottom of the quirk.

Along the inside edge of the stiles drive a nail through the face frame into each of the shelves. You can conceal these nails by toenailing them from the edge of the board inside the door opening. Set the nails and cover them with wood putty.

Now, trim the bottoms of the stiles flush with the sides. Lay out the curved cutouts for the legs next. The cutout on the side comes very close to the bottom shelf. Make sure that you leave at least ⅛ inch between the bottom of the shelf and the top of the cutout. Make the cutout with a coping saw or a sabre saw. Smooth up the saw cuts with a spokeshave. Start at the top of the curve and pull the spokeshave towards the bottom (Illus. 8-21).

The Door Frame

Begin work on the door frame by ripping the boards to width. Make the door stiles (Part F in Illus. 8-2) about ¹⁄₁₆ inch wider than necessary. This will allow you to do the final fitting of the door with a plane after the door is assembled. Cut the rails to length, allowing for the length of the tenons. Cut the stiles to length, adding 2 inches extra. This extra length is called a horn; it supports the mortise as you chop it by hand. After assembly, cut it off.

Now, set up a plow plane to plow the grooves in the frame members. Install a ¼-inch-wide cutter.

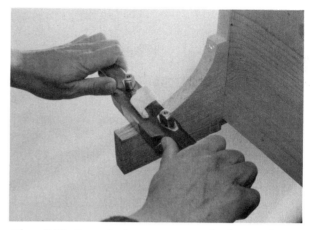

Illus. 8-21. Smooth the saw cuts on the legs with a spokeshave. Start at the top of the curve and pull the spokeshave towards the bottom.

Set the fence to place the groove ¼ inch away from the rear edge. This will place the groove off center. The bead on the front will weaken the front of the groove, so the groove is placed off center to allow extra thickness on the front to compensate for the strength lost by cutting the bead. Set the depth stop for ⅜ inch. Now, plow the grooves as described in Chapter 4. Note that the center rail is grooved on both edges.

Set up the universal combination plane to cut a ⅜-inch bead. The setup is the same as used to cut the bead on the face frame stiles described earlier. Bead along the inside edge of the front face on the door stiles and rails (Illus. 8-22). The center rail is beaded on both edges.

Illus. 8-22. Use a universal combination plane to cut a ⅜-inch bead on the door frame members.

Illus. 8-23. You must cut away the bead on the stiles in the joint area. To do this, make a mitre jig that can be clamped over the stiles.

Illus. 8-24. Make the tenons with a fillister. Place all three of the rails edge to edge and clamp them to the bench.

Before you can chop the mortises, you must cut away the bead in the area of the joint. To do this, make a mitre jig that can be clamped over the stiles. The jig should be cut to exactly 45 degrees. Make some test cuts on scrap first, to make sure that the jig is accurate. Then place the jig over the stile and position it carefully (Illus. 8-23). Rest the blade of a backsaw on the jig and saw through the stile until the cut is flush with the far side of the quirk on the bead.

Now, use a chisel to cut away the waste, leaving a smooth, flat joint area where both the bead and the groove have been completely removed. Lay out the mortises with a marking gauge. The mortises are ⅜ inch wide and centered on the stile. Chop the mortises with a mortise chisel to a depth of 1¼ inches.

The tenons are cut with the fillister. Place all three of the rails edge to edge and clamp them to the bench. Make sure that their ends are lined up with each other. If there is any difference in the length of the rails, score a line across the ends and plane the ends with a block or smooth plane until they are all equal. Work in from both edges, to prevent splintering. Lay out the tenons with a marking gauge and score the shoulder mark deeply with a knife. Now, plane down the cheeks of the tenons using the same procedure described earlier for the top face-frame rail (Illus. 8-24).

Trim the tenons with a backsaw so that they fit the mortises. Mitre the end of the bead using the mitre jig and a backsaw. Make a test assembly of the door frame. You can make adjustments to the

fit of the joints by trimming the tenon shoulders with a shoulder plane. If it is necessary to trim the mitres, you can use the mitre jig as a shooting board to guide a shoulder plane that has a removable toe (see Illus. 4-4). This exposes the plane iron at the front of the plane and makes it possible to plane right into the corner of the mitre.

With this type of beaded door, the panels are simply rabbeted to fit into the groove on the frame. The panels are ⅝ inch thick. Cut the panel to its correct size first. During periods of high humidity, the panels will absorb moisture and swell. This will cause the panels to become wider than they are during periods of low humidity. The height of the panels won't change much because the orientation of the wood fibres causes expansion to take place, mostly across their width. This means that the height of the panel can be exactly the same as the distance between the bottom of the grooves in the rails. The width of the panel should be ¼ inch less than the distance between the bottoms of the grooves in the stiles. This will leave ⅛-inch clearance on each side to allow the panel to expand during periods of high humidity.

Gauge a line ¼ inch from the back of the panel on all four edges. Make the rabbets on the top and bottom edges of the panels first. The cross-grain rabbets on both panels can be cut at the same time. Clamp the two panels edge to edge on the bench and add a backup board to the far edge of the panels at the toe end. Turn down the nicker on the plane and set the fence to make a ½-inch-wide rabbet. Plane across the ends of the panels until you reach the gauged line. Then turn the panels around and make the rabbets on the other end.

To make the rabbets on the sides of the panels, turn the nicker back up and reset the fence to make a ⅜-inch-wide rabbet. Making this rabbet narrower helps to keep the quirk between the panel and the bead equal to the quirk at the top and bottom of the panel.

Now, plane the rabbet on the sides of the panels. If necessary, you can clean up the shoulders of the rabbets with a shoulder rabbet plane.

Now, assemble the door. Carefully apply glue to the mortise-and-tenon joints. Don't use too much glue, because it can squeeze out into the panel groove and glue the panel in place. This can eventually cause the panel to split. The panel must be free to move in the groove as the moisture content of the wood changes with variations in air humidity.

Clamp the door together with bar clamps, and then drill the holes for the ¼-inch dowels that lock the mortise-and-tenon joints together. Drive the dowels into the holes and let the glue dry. After the glue has set, use a sharp chisel to trim the dowels close to the surface of the door. Then trim them flush with a block plane.

Trim off the horns of the stiles so that they are flush with the top and bottom rails. Place the door on the face frame and note how much the door needs to be trimmed. Use a jack plane, a jointer, or a trying plane to trim the door to fit the opening. When the door is close to its correct size, tip the plane so it slopes to the inside of the door at

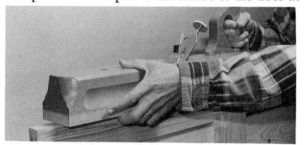

Illus. 8-25. Use a jack plane, a jointer, or a trying plane to trim the door to fit the opening. When the door is close to its correct size, tip the plane so that it slopes to the inside of the door at about a five-degree angle. Plane both edges of the door at this angle.

about a five-degree angle. Plane both edges of the door to this angle (Illus. 8-25). Bevelling the door like this allows you to fit the door closer to the stiles of the face frame than you could if you left the edges square. The high side of the bevel on the face of the door fits close to the face-frame stile, but the bevelled edge allows enough clearance for the door to open without rubbing against the stile.

Using Cornice Moulding

Apply the cornice moulding to the top of the cupboard after assembling the carcass but before installing the back. Making this moulding gives you a chance to explore many of the capabilities of a universal combination plane.

The cornice moulding can be cut using any of the planes described in Chapter 6. It can be made a little more easily with a Stanley #55 plane, but it can still be cut even with the Record 045C plane. Cut the moulding on a single long board. Then cut the parts to length and mitre the corners. You will need a piece of 1½-inch-thick pine about 3½ inches wide and 72 inches long. The extra width makes it easier to clamp the board to the bench, and the extra length allows you some leeway when you cut the parts, so you can cut out areas where a change in grain direction caused some chipping or other defects in the moulding.

Clamp the board to the bench with its edge overhanging the bench slightly. There are many steps involved in making this moulding. The first cut is made close to the far side, and the subsequent cuts are made progressively closer to the edge closer to you. All of the fence distances given in these directions are measured from the edge of the board to the cutter edge nearer the fence.

The first cut is made with a ⅜-inch plow cutter, and with the fence set to 2⅛ inches. Plow this groove ¼ inch deep. Next, install a ½-inch bead cutter. With the fence set to 1⅝ inches, cut a bead (Illus. 8-26). As soon as the bead is fully rounded and the quirk is flush with the groove made previously, stop the cut.

Illus. 8-26. Making the cornice moulding gives you a chance to explore many of the capabilities of a universal combination plane. Here, I'm using a Record 045C plane to make the first bead.

Illus. 8-27. Before proceeding with the next moulding cut, you have to remove a lot of waste wood. You can remove most of the excess wood with a jack plane.

Illus. 8-28. A Stanley #55 plane can make the cove and bead in a single step.

Illus. 8-29. You can make the cove and bead separately, if you don't have a Stanley #55 plane. Here I'm using a Record 045C plane to make the bead.

Now, reinstall the ⅜-inch plow cutter and, with the fence set to 1¼ inches, plow a groove. Stop the cut when the bottom of the groove is flush with the quirk of the bead. Reset the fence to 1⅛ inches and plow another groove ½ inch deep.

Before proceeding with the next cut, you have to remove a lot of waste wood. You can remove most of the excess wood with a jack plane. Gauge a line along the edge of the board ⅝ inch up from the bottom. Now, set the jack plane to make a rank cut and plane down the area between the last groove and the edge. As the plane gets close to the bottom of the groove, start to tilt the plane (Illus. 8-27). Stop cutting when the sole of the plane is touching the bottom of the groove and the gauged line.

If you have a Stanley #55 plane, you can complete the moulding with one more cut. Several more steps are required if you are using one of the other planes. To use the Stanley #55 plane, install the #116 cutter. This cutter makes a 1-inch cove and a ¼-inch bead. Set the fence so that the bead is ⅛ inch away from the edge of the board (Illus. 8-28). Stop cutting when the moulding is ½ inch thick at its thinnest part.

Cove cutters won't work in the other planes because the sole runners can't be adjusted vertically, but it is possible to cut a cove using a fluting cutter. Before using the fluting cutter, it is best to remove more of the waste wood. Install a ⅜-inch plow cutter and plow a groove ½ inch from the edge. Plow this groove until the thickness of the wood between the back of the moulding and the bottom of the groove is ½ inch. Now, install the ¾-inch fluting cutter. Set the fence so that the sole runner of the plane will ride just past the far shoulder of the groove you just made. Stop planing when the cove forms a smooth transition with the bottom of the groove.

Install the ¼-inch beading cutter in the plane and set the fence to place the bead ⅛ inch away from the edge. Stop planing when the quirk of the bead is flush with the cove (Illus. 8-29). There will be some waste left between the bead and the edge of the board; use a fillister to remove this waste. The final step is to rip the moulding to a 2¼-inch width.

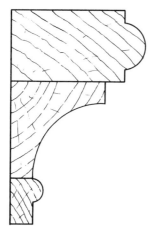

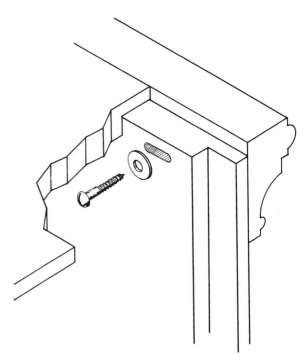

Illus. 8-30. For those who would like to build this project but don't have a plane capable of making the cove, you can make the moulding using a piece of commercial cove moulding, as shown here.

Illus. 8-31. The grain in the moulding runs at a 90-degree angle to the grain in the sides and top. If the cornice were rigidly attached to the side, changes in wood moisture content could cause the sides to split or the mitre joint to pull loose. To solve this problem, attach the cornice with screws in elongated holes; this holds the moulding in place while allowing the sides and top to shrink and swell freely.

The fluting cutters don't come with the standard set of cutters supplied with the plane. For those of you who would like to build this project without buying an optional cutter, here is an alternate method of making the moulding (Illus. 8-30). Buy a piece of commercially made cove moulding. Then cut a ½-inch bead on the edge of a ¾-inch-thick board to make the top part of the moulding. Next, cut a ¼-inch bead on a piece of ½-inch-thick wood. This creates the bottom bead. Both of the beads will be easier to cut if you use a wide board and rip it to its required width after the bead is made. Now, glue the beaded boards to the cove moulding.

Install the cornice on the front of the cupboard first. Since the grain of the moulding runs in the same direction as the grain on the top piece, this moulding can be securely fastened along its full length. Apply glue to the back of the moulding and position it on the front of the cupboard. You can attach it with finish nails or, if you would like to eliminate any visible fasteners, attach it with screws driven from the inside of the cabinet through the face frame. Keep the screws as close to the top as possible, so that they will drive into the thick part of the moulding.

Now, cut the side pieces. Check the fit of the mitres. If necessary, you can trim the mitres with a block plane to adjust the fit. The grain in the moulding runs at a 90-degree angle to the grain in

the sides and top. If the cornice were rigidly attached to the side, changes in wood moisture content could cause the sides to split or the mitre joint to pull loose. To solve this problem, attach the cornice with screws in elongated holes. This holds the moulding in place while allowing the sides and top to shrink and swell freely.

Begin by drilling the screw holes. Three screws are used on each side. The one closest to the front is not slotted. The center hole and the rear hole are slotted to allow for wood movement (Illus. 8-31).

To make the slotted holes, drill two holes about ½ inch apart and saw out the wood between the holes with a coping saw. Now, apply glue to the mitre joint and the first 4 inches of the back of the moulding. Place it on the cabinet and drive the front screw through the side and into the back of the moulding. Use roundhead screws with washers for the slotted holes. Place the screw in the middle of the slot, to allow for wood movement in either direction.

Tongue-and-Groove Joints for the Back

The back is made from narrow boards that are joined together with tongue-and-groove joints. This arrangement allows for shrinking and swelling in the wood without causing splits in the boards. No glue is used on the tongue-and-groove joints, leaving them free to slide in and out as the boards dry out or absorb moisture from the air.

Make the grooves first with a ³⁄₁₆-inch plow cutter in the universal combination plane, and then use the ³⁄₁₆-inch tongue cutter to cut the tongues (Illus. 8-32). Refer to Chapter 6 for detailed directions on setting up the plane and cutting the tongues and grooves.

Note that there should be one board that only has a tongue and one board that only has a groove. These are the first and last boards of the panel. They will fit in the rabbets in the sides.

Make a trial assembly of the back and check its overall width. The dimensions for the back boards given in the bill of materials will result in a panel that is about ¼ inch too wide. Trim the first and last boards to bring the panel to its correct size. Attach the back boards with brass flathead wood screws. Position one screw in the middle of the top and bottom of each board and one in the middle of the board that will be attached to the second shelf. You can also add a few screws along the sides to attach the back to the sides of the carcass, but don't add any other screws to the rest of the back boards. When you place the screws in the middle of each board, the board is free to shrink and swell with changes in humidity.

Final Details

The cupboard is now fully assembled, except for the door. Cut gains (recesses) for the hinges with a chisel and make a trial fit of all of the hardware. Now, remove the hardware and give the wood a final smoothing before you apply the finish. You can use a finishing plane or a scraper to remove any plane marks or other imperfections in the surface (Illus. 8-33).

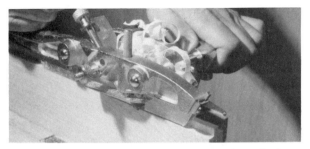

Illus. 8-32. The back consists of narrow boards that are joined together with tongue-and-groove joints. Make the grooves first with a ³⁄₁₆-inch plow cutter in the universal combination plane. Then use the ³⁄₁₆-inch tongue cutter to cut the tongues, as shown here.

Illus. 8-33. A cabinet scraper can be used for the final smoothing of the wood.

It is possible to achieve a perfectly smooth surface with planes and scrapers alone, but if you feel it is necessary, you can sand the surface with fine sandpaper. The degree of smoothing required depends on personal taste and the style of the project. On a "country" project, you may want to leave very visible indications that a hand plane was used. Even on more finished antiques, plane marks are usually visible on hidden surfaces such as shelf bottoms and drawer bottoms. On my version of this Shaker jelly cupboard, I have left a few traces of plane marks on the outside, to give it an antique look. For the inside of the cupboard, I used a smooth plane on the tops of the shelves and left the marks from the trying plane visible on the shelf bottoms.

Now that you have read through this chapter, you should have a better understanding of how the various planes described in the earlier chapters are all used in conjunction with each other to complete a project. If you actually build this project, you will gain practical experience with most of the basic planing skills.

GLOSSARY

Astragal A narrow, half-round moulding.

Backing Off The process of removing the wire edge on a plane blade. The back of the iron rests flat on the face of a fine stone, and the fine stone is used to back off the iron.

Backlash The slack or play in the adjustment mechanism of the plane.

Baller A tool used to round over the end of a dowel.

Bareface Joint A joint in which one or more of its shoulders are eliminated. (See Shoulder.)

Bead A traditional decoration often used with a tongue-and-groove joint to hide the gap between the boards.

Bedding Angle The angle at which the frog or bed of the plane holds the plane iron.

Bench Planes Planes used to smooth the face and edges of a board. They are the most common types of plane.

Bevel The inside surface that is sharpened on a plane blade.

Block Planes Small planes that fit into the palm of your hand. They are used primarily for trimming.

Boxing The process of adding a new piece of wood to the front of the mouth of the plane.

Burnish To polish or form a burr edge on a hard tool by rubbing it with another hard tool.

Cabinet Scraper A scraper with a cast-iron body that holds a scraper blade.

Camber A slight convexity, arch, or curvature.

Carcass The basic box or frame of a cabinet.

Chamfer A bevelled cut on an edge.

Cheek The part of the joint that is parallel with the face or edge.

Clearance Angle The angle formed between the work and the underside of the cutting edge of the blade.

Combination Plane Any plane that can be used for more than one job.

Common Pitch Refers to a plane iron held at 45 degrees to the work by the frog or bed.

Compass Plane A plane used to make convex or concave shapes.

Cove A concave moulding cut into the edge of the board.

Cutting Angle The angle formed between the work and the top of the blade.

Dado Joint A T-shaped joint that is used to make boxes, cabinets, and shelves.

Dress To improve or smooth the surface of the wood.

Fillet A flat section on a moulding used to separate a section of the moulding.

Fillister A rabbet plane with a fence and depth stop.

Fine Setting The setting of a plane iron (blade) that will make a shallow cut.

Fluting A decorative moulding that is frequently used as a decoration on table legs. It has a concave half-round profile.

Fore Plane A plane about 18 inches long used to surface or dress rough lumber.

Grain The orientation of the fibres in the wood, or a term used to describe the visible pattern of pores and growth rings on a board.

Grinding The coarse wearing away of a softer material by the abrasive actions of a harder material.

Gutter Plane A plane with a convex sole and iron that can be used to make large architectural mouldings such as the cove moulding.

Hand Scraper A very simple scraper that consists of a steel blade that is held in your hands.

High Spots Areas of the board that are thicker or wider than the rest of the board.

Hogging Off Making deep, rough cuts in wood with a plane.

Hollow-Ground Iron A hollow-ground iron has a bevel face that is slightly concave.

Hollows and Rounds The simplest types of moulding planes. The hollow plane has a concave profile. The round plane has a convex profile.

Honing Giving a keen edge to a plane iron.

Hook Angle The angle of the blade's cutting edge as it relates to the centerline of the blade.

Jack Plane A plane 12 to 17 inches long that is used to remove saw marks from lumber and cut down high spots.

Jointer A plane 22 to 36 inches long that is designed to make an edge straight and square with the face of the board.

Jointing Making an edge straight and square with the face of the board.

Match Planes Planes used to make tongue-and-groove joints. These planes are used in pairs. One plane cuts the tongue. The other plane cuts the groove.

Metallic Planes Planes that are made almost entirely of metal.

Microbevels Small, secondary bevels at the tip of the plane iron.

Mitre Joint A joint that is cut at an angle. When two boards meet at 90 degrees, the mitre angle is 45 degrees.

Mortise-and-Tenon Joint A joint in which a projection called a tenon on one board fits into a pocket called a mortise in the other board.

Moulding Planes Planes used to make mouldings.

Mouldings Decorative recessed or relieved surfaces.

Ogee A moulding with an S-shaped profile.

Ovolo A rounded convex moulding.

Panel-Raising Plane A plane used to make the bevelled edges of a panel. Panel-raising planes are often called fielding planes.

Pointer A tool used to taper the end of a dowel.

Quirk The small groove that defines the edges of the bead.

Rabbet Joint A corner joint with one shoulder. It is often used to join the top of the cabinet to its sides, and to attach the back of the cabinet.

Rabbet Plane A plane with an iron that extends to the edge of the sole.

Radius Plane A plane used to round or chamfer the edges of a board.

Rake Angle The angle formed between the top of the cutting edge and a line perpendicular to the work surface.

Rank Setting The setting of a plane iron (blade) that will make a heavy cut.

Reed A series of beads cut side by side.

Rounder A tool used to make dowels or round stock.

Router Plane A plane used to smooth the bottom of a recess, which is a cut indentation in a piece of wood.

Sash Planes A special moulding plane used to make windows.

Scraper A tool used for the final smoothing of wood.

Scratch Stock A scraping tool used to cut mouldings.

Scrub Plane A short jack plane generally used to rough-out wood close to its final dimensions and to remove large bumps and warps in the board.

Sharpening Angle The angle that you hold the blade at while you hone it on a whetstone.

Shooting Boards Boards with straight, true edges that are used to guide the plane.

Shoulder The part of the joint that is cut 90 degrees to the face or edge of the board. A joint only has a shoulder when that part of the board that fits into a joint must be thinner or narrower than the rest of the board.

Skew To set something at an angle.

Slipstone A small whetstone that is rounded or tapered.

Smooth Plane A plane 9 or 10 inches long used to smooth the surface of a board.

Spokeshave A tool, originally used to smooth wooden wheel spokes, that is very useful today for smoothing the sculpted shapes of modern furniture.

Sprung Plane A plane that can be held at an angle of 15 to 30 degrees.

Stick The board that the moulding is cut into.

Sticking or Striking The process of cutting mouldings.

Stropping A process sometimes used when sharpening a plane blade in which a piece of leather that is impregnated with a fine abrasive is used to make the cutting edge very sharp.

Tear-Out A condition that occurs when the grain of a board changes direction and the plane blade starts to chip the wood.

Temper The correct heat treatment of a tool's metal, to make it stay sharp longer.

Tongue-and-Groove Joint A two-part joint in which a projection on one board called a tongue fits into a groove on the other board.

Traditional Planes Planes with a wood body and a blade held in place with a wood wedge.

Transitional Planes Planes that have wood bodies, but have metal working parts that are used to secure and adjust the plane.

Trying Planes Planes 20 to 24 inches long used to flatten the surface of a board and remove the marks left by the jack on the fore plane.

Tuning The process of adjusting all of the working parts of a plane to their optimum positions and removing all imperfections in the casting left from the manufacturing process.

Universal Plane Any plane that can be used with cutters of different sizes.

Whetstones Abrasive stones used to sharpen edge tools.

York Pitch A reference to a blade bedded at a high 50-degree angle.

Index